ECHO
OF THE ELEPHANTS

ECHO
OF THE ELEPHANTS

The Story of an Elephant Family

Cynthia Moss

Photographs by Martyn Colbeck

William Morrow and Company, Inc.
New York

For Marion
whose enthusiasm, talent
and friendship
touched so many of us

First published in Great Britain in 1992 by BBC Books, a division of BBC Enterprises, Ltd.

Library of Congress Cataloging-in-Publication Data

Moss, Cynthia.
    Echo of the elephants : the story of an elephant family / Cynthia
Moss.
       p.   cm.
    ISBN 0-688-12103-9
    1. Echo (Elephant)   2. African elephant—Kenya—Amboseli National
Park—Behavior.   3. African elephant—Kenya—Amboseli National Park—
Biography.   I. Title.
    QL737.P98M667   1993
    599.6'1'096762—dc20
                                    92-33463
                                    CIP

Printed in the United States of America

2   3   4   5   6   7   8   9   10

CONTENTS

ACKNOWLEDGEMENTS

Marion Zunz had a passion for life in its many forms. The natural world inspired and delighted her and no animal more so than the elephant. It was long her dream to make a behaviour film about African elephants based on the long-term research findings of the Amboseli Elephant Research Project. As only Marion could do, she persisted, gently but persuasively, for 10 years and finally her dream became a reality. In January 1990, with Marion as producer, we began a two-and-a-half-year project to make a film about the Amboseli elephants. Apart from two trips to Kenya, Marion encouraged us and followed our progress from the frustratingly distant BBC offices. Nevertheless, she got as involved with the EBs, 'our family', as we were. Marion did not live to see the final version of the film or book. She was killed in a skiing accident on 5 January 1992. It was Marion's energy, her intelligence, her unique off-beat view of things, her humour, and most of all her commitment that created the film and made this book possible. We have dedicated the book to Marion in appreciation for all that she did and was.

A film is always a team effort, and even a book, although apparently a more solitary undertaking, relies on the work of others. Many people and organisations helped us over the two and a half years of filming, post-production, writing and editing. First on the film production side we would like to thank the following for their invaluable contribution and support: David Attenborough, Martin Elsbury, Angela Groves, Christina Hamilton, David Heeley, John Heminway, Lesley Jones, Fred Kaufman, Ginny Lucas, Cathy McConnell, Linda Romano, Mike Rosenberg, Mike Salisbury, Marney Shears and John Sparks. The book benefited greatly from the efforts of the following: Sheila Ableman, Nicky Copeland, Harvey Ginsberg, Tim Higgins, Frank Phillips, Anthony Sheil

and Wendy Weil. We are also grateful to Jane Harvey and Chris Elworthy of Canon UK Ltd, Mecca Ibrahim of Fuji Professional and David Cottam of Fuji Film Processing for their generosity and skills, and to Wayne Esarove and Zenith Datasystems for their invaluable support.

Africa is not the easiest of continents to work on, but it has the friendliest and most helpful people. We could not have carried out our project without the aid of the authorities and our many friends and colleagues. We would first like to express our appreciation to the Ministry of Information and Broadcasting of the Government of Kenya for allowing us to film in the country, and to Richard Leakey and Joseph Mburugu of Kenya Wildlife Service for permission to work in Amboseli National Park. In Amboseli itself we owe a debt of gratitude to Warden Naftali Kio and Assistant Warden Michael Kipkeu for their hospitality and support.

In Nairobi we greatly appreciated the backing of a number of people: Billy Dhillon of Movietone Productions, Alison and Peter Cadot and the African Wildlife Foundation office, particularly Mark Stanley Price and Deborah Snelson. In addition, we also appreciated the enthusiasm and encouragement of Elizabeth McCorkle and Diana McMeekin of the AWF, Washington.

Our colleagues on the Amboseli Research Project and our companions in the camp were a source of encouragement and kindness and we would like to thank: Kadzo Kangwana, Wambua Kativa, Phyllis Lee, Keith Lindsay, Hamisi Mutinda, Peter Ngandi, Norah Wamaitha Njiraini, Joyce Poole, Deborah Ross, Soila Sayialel and Catherine Sayialel.

Finally, we would like to thank Conrad Hirsh and Heather, Josephine and Emily Colbeck: Conrad for providing an abundance of moral and material support in the form of supplies, communications, companionship, and, perhaps most important, his rescuing of us during the all too frequent vehicle breakdowns and disasters; and Heather and the girls for keeping the home fires burning and for their remarkable tolerance and patience during Martyn's long absences.

Cynthia Moss   Martyn Colbeck

FOREWORD

by Sir David Attenborough

I wonder if anyone has ever known a wild, free-roaming elephant as well as Cynthia Moss knows Echo. The two have been in one another's company for over 20 years now, sometimes for days and weeks on end. As Cynthia has watched, Echo has guided her family through good times and bad, finding food for them during famines, leading them on migration along traditional pathways, giving birth to her own calves and helping her sisters and daughters with the birth of theirs.

There was a time, not so long ago, when such a relationship between an animal and a zoologist would have been regarded with deep suspicion by orthodox science. For one thing, it might lead to an emotional attachment that could endanger scientific objectivity. Worse, it could result in that ultimate sin of the behavioural scientist, the unwarranted attribution to an animal of human motives and emotions. In any case, such arguments used to run, science should generalise not particularise.

Then things began to change. Watching animals in cages running round mazes and solving problems devised for them by experimenters became less fashionable. Zoologists abandoned their laboratories and moved out into the field to discover how animals

---

Overleaf: *A mother, her calf, and a younger female helper (all members of a larger family) head towards their night feeding and resting area as the sun sets. The matriarchal family unit is the basis of elephant society.*

behaved in their natural environments. There they realised that many questions could not be answered unless animals could be recognised as individuals. To do that, they used labels of some kind – collars around the neck, rings on the legs, even numbers tattooed or burnt on an animal's flank. This took time, was very laborious and might even endanger an animal's well-being, so it was difficult to do on a large scale. But a new generation of field-workers, with the keen observational powers of gifted naturalists, detected that individuals of many species varied enough in tiny physical details for them all to be recognised without having to interfere with them in any way.

That advance transformed the science of animal behaviour. As soon as observers began to follow particular animals over any length of time, they discovered that many of the generalisations made so confidently before were simply not true. All individuals of a species do not necessarily behave in the same way. Attributing particular characters to different animals is not always unjustified anthropomorphism. It may be an accurate assessment of the reality and bring a new understanding of the lives of many species.

No one animal could exemplify this more clearly than Echo. Her character emerges as vividly from these pages as might that of a human subject from a perceptive biography. And no longer is it a scientific slur to say such a thing. On the contrary, it is a tribute to Cynthia Moss's patience and insight as an observer. She has demonstrated that a scientist can be both objective and – using the word in its most literal sense – compassionate.

Today, elephants are in great peril. They are the biggest of all living land animals and as such they need great areas in which to roam and much vegetation on which to feed. In the increasingly crowded continent of Africa, there are more and more competitors for such things. To make matters worse, elephants carry in their jaws a treasure so valuable that there is a great deal of money to be made by killing them. If elephants are to survive, human beings will have to be convinced that these magnificent, intelligent creatures are entitled to retain some share of the living space left on earth. There could be no more persuasive argument for them than that provided by Cynthia Moss – and Echo – in this brilliant, perceptive and enchanting book.

INTRODUCTION

Echo is not a particularly tall elephant nor is she perfectly proportioned, but nonetheless she is very beautiful. Her long, graceful tusks curve together and cross at the tips, and when she walks, she swings her head and tusks from side to side in a pleasing rhythm with her footsteps. Echo is the serene and gentle matriarch of a family of elephants that lives in Amboseli National Park in southern Kenya.

This book is Echo's story: it is an attempt to open a window into the life of one elephant family over a period of 18 months from January 1990 to June 1991. During many of those months, Martyn Colbeck and I followed, observed, photographed and filmed Echo and her relatives for a BBC documentary film on elephant behaviour.

Amboseli

Echo's family, known by the codename 'EB', is one of 50 elephant families that live in and around Amboseli National Park. It is a small park by African standards, only 390 square

Overleaf: *Kilimanjaro dominates the landscape and ecology of Amboseli: rain falling on the mountain filters down into underground aquifers and surfaces in the Park in the form of springs, streams, swamps and pools, providing both food and water for an abundance of wildlife.*

kilometres (150 square miles), and much of it is the seasonally flooded bed of Lake Amboseli, which dried up 10 000 years ago. Receiving only about 300 millimetres (12 inches) of rain a year, the park should be a desert and the old lake bed does look as dead and dry as the Sahara for most of the year. Yet Amboseli is one of the richest wildlife areas in Kenya for the snows of Kilimanjaro glisten less than 40 kilometres (25 miles) away. Towering over the surrounding landscape at 5895 metres (19 340 feet), Kilimanjaro provides the lifeblood of Amboseli, continuously feeding the swamps and springs in the park with thousands of litres per minute of fresh, clear water carried in underground aquifers. The combination of low rainfall and underground streams makes the landscape of Amboseli a study of contrasts, with bare, dusty plains suddenly giving way to trees, papyrus and lush green swampland.

Amboseli's swamps and springs have been used by wildlife and humans and their domestic animals for hundreds of years. For the last 400–500 years, the area has been held by the Maasai tribe, fierce warriors and pastoralists who do not hunt wild animals for meat or trophies. The Maasai have lived in remarkable harmony with wildlife and, as a result, the best places to see wild animals in East Africa are those held by the Maasai. The oral history of the Maasai indicates that they have been sharing the Amboseli swamps with wildlife since they first arrived. Traditionally the Maasai and the migratory herbivores – elephants, buffaloes, wildebeests, zebras and gazelles – concentrate around the swamps in the dry season and disperse to outlying areas in the wet season. The dispersal area is almost 10 times as large as the park itself, up to 3000 square kilometres (1200 square miles), and without it the animals could not exist in the numbers that they do.

The Amboseli area has been visited by tourists since the 1930s and by hunters even before that. The wildlife was known to be easy to photograph and to shoot. In 1974, much of the central area around the swamps was declared a national park and the Maasai were asked to leave. In return they were given compensation in the form of a water pipeline and direct revenue. It has not been a completely successful arrangement, and periodically the Maasai spear elephants, rhinos and other large species, which is a traditional means

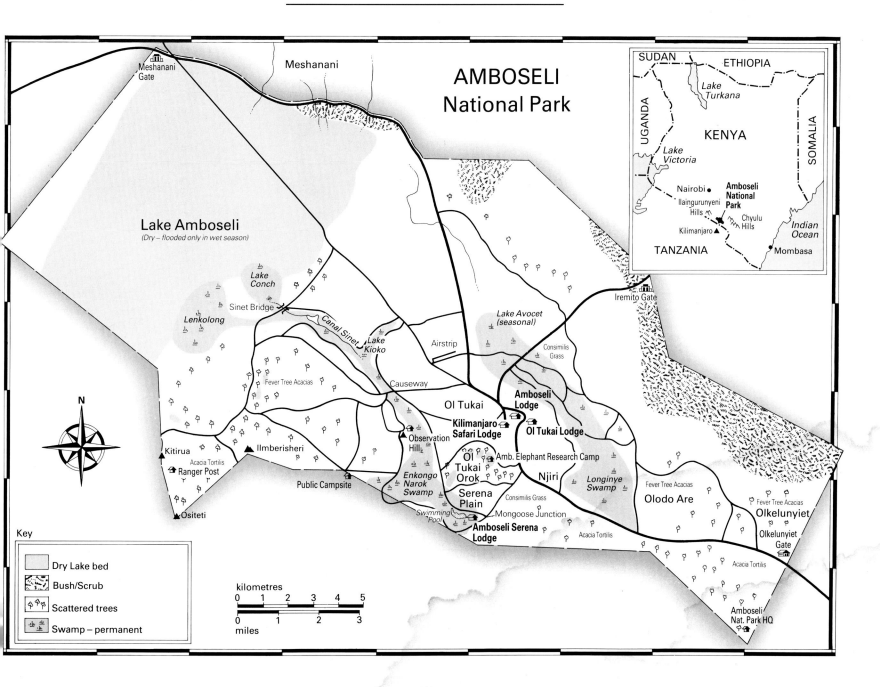

AMBOSELI
National Park

Meshanani Gate

Meshanani

SUDAN **ETHIOPIA**

UGANDA

Lake Turkana

KENYA

Lake Victoria

Nairobi ●   **Amboseli National Park**

Ilaingurunyeni Hills

Chyulu Hills

Kilimanjaro ▲

Indian Ocean

TANZANIA

● Mombasa

SOMALIA

Lake Amboseli
(Dry – flooded only in wet season)

Lake Conch

Sinet Bridge

Lenkolong

Canal Sinet

Lake Kioko

Iremito Gate

Lake Avocet (seasonal)

Airstrip

Consimilis Grass

Fever Tree Acacias

Causeway

Ol Tukai

Amboseli Lodge

Kilimanjaro Safari Lodge

Ol Tukai Lodge

Observation Hill

Amb. Elephant Research Camp

Kitirua

Acacia Tortilis

Ranger Post

▲ Ilmberisheri

Ol Tukai Orok

Njiri

Longinye Swamp

Enkongo Narok Swamp

Public Campsite

Serena Plain

Consimilis Grass

Olodo Are

Fever Tree Acacias

Fever Tree Acacias

▲ Ositeti

Swimming Pool

Mongoose Junction

Amboseli Serena Lodge

Acacia Tortilis

Olkelunyiet

Olkelunyiet Gate

Acacia Tortilis

Amboseli Nat. Park HQ

Key

	Dry Lake bed
	Bush/Scrub
	Scattered trees
	Swamp – permanent

kilometres

0 1 2 3 4 5

0 1 2 3

miles

N

Above and below:
*Elephants generally drink once a day, although
in some seasons and in some habitats they can
adapt to drinking every other day or even every
third day. In Amboseli there is always enough water
and, therefore, drinking sessions are relaxed
and companionable occasions.*

*Mr Nick, an adult male in his mid-30s, moves across one of the large
open pans in Amboseli. Males leave their families at around
14 years old to lead independent lives spending much of their time
on their own or in the company of a few other males.*

of proving their bravery and, more recently, a form of political protest. Fortunately the incidents are relatively rare, and Amboseli continues to have an abundance of approachable and relaxed animals. It is also one of the few areas in all of Africa where elephants have not been under heavy pressure from poachers, mainly because the Maasai will not tolerate outsiders coming in to kill their wildlife.

The Amboseli Elephant Research Project

The elephants of Amboseli are now the best known in Africa, having been the subjects of a detailed, long-term study which I initiated in September 1972 and have been directing ever since. I chose the Amboseli elephants for study because they were one of the last relatively undisturbed populations in Africa. My goal from the beginning was to collect basic information on elephants that were neither compressed into a small protected area nor heavily poached as most populations across the continent were. I hoped that data on elephants functioning in a fairly natural ecosystem, responding primarily to environmental rather than human-made pressures, would aid assessments of the status of less fortunate populations elsewhere. Sadly, the intensive poaching of the 1980s has made this role of the Amboseli project invaluable.

The Amboseli project is now in its twentieth year. With the help of colleagues, students and research assistants, I have been able to keep the study going continuously. Over 1200 elephants have been identified individually and each has been assigned a name, number or code. There are currently 755 living members, and well over half of these are known-aged – that is, their birth dates have been recorded to within one month. Their mothers and maternal sisters, brothers, aunts, uncles, nieces, nephews, and cousins are also known. Fathers and paternal relatives are more difficult to determine. Nevertheless, this fund of information on the histories and relatedness of the Amboseli elephants forms a unique body of knowledge for a wildlife population. It also makes watching them as fascinating as following a soap opera or reading an intricate family saga.

Elephant cows and their calves live in family units, which in Amboseli average about 11 members. A family consists of related adult females and their offspring, ranging from newborn calves to adolescent males and females up to about 10 or 11 years old. Families are tight-knit with strong bonds between the adult females. Each family is led by the oldest female – the matriarch. Female calves grow up and stay with the family, and may start producing their own calves at 12 or 13 years of age. Males leave the family soon after reaching sexual maturity at about 14 years old. They are then referred to as 'independent bulls'. Unlike the females, the bulls form only loose and temporary associations with each other. Usually it is the bulls over 30 years old who mate with the cows and father the calves.

In the Amboseli study, I catalogued males and females in different ways because of their different social lives. Since bulls do not form permanent groupings, each male has to be filed as an individual. Males have been assigned a number starting with the first bull that was photographed, M1. The numbers currently go up to M454 and are recorded on computer data sheets. There are presently 177 adult bulls, most of which have been given names as well. Females are filed according to family, and each family has an alphabetical letter code. At the beginning of the study, I assigned single letters to families but when I got to 27 I had to switch to a two-letter code, such as AA, AB, BA and BB. Each female is given a name starting with her family letter. Thus the AA family includes females named Amy, Abigail, Amelia and so on. For the data records, their names are shortened to a three-letter code, AMY, ABI, AME, etc. In Amboseli, the 50 family units are made up of 578 cows and calves.

Overleaf: *The EB family at rest with nine of the members visible (from left to right) Echo, Ella, Eric, Ewan, Edgar, Enid, Eliot, Eudora and Erin. At the beginning of 1990, the family numbered 14, which is just above average size for the 50 family units in Amboseli.*

Our knowledge of the 50 families is not uniform, the histories of some having been followed in more detail than others. The best known are among the 30 or so families that spend much of their time in the central part of Amboseli, concentrating in and around the two major swamps – Longinye and Enkongo Narok. The other 20 spend more time in areas peripheral to the park and are seen less often. All the researchers who have worked on the project have families (and bulls) that they prefer to others. The preference depends partly on how easy a family is to find and follow. However, there is often a far less concrete and objective element: some families are simply more appealing than others. I think our response is related to a family's general behaviour and, not surprisingly, to the character of the matriarch.

The EB Family

When I asked several of my colleagues which family they would choose if they were going to concentrate on only one for a film, they all said the AAs, the EBs or the JAs, and of those their first choice would be the EBs. Having already narrowed the choice down to the same three families and selected the EBs myself, I tried to analyse what it was about these families that made them come to mind for all of us. First, each had a fairly regular pattern of movement and thus would be relatively easy to follow on a daily basis. In addition, the EBs were very habituated to our vehicles, even to the point of being 'friendly' and going out of their way to approach them. Finally, all three families had matriarchs that were striking looking and highly 'likable'. This may seem an odd word to use, but elephants do have strong personalities that are easily discernible. While our rigorous, quantitative data collection methods allow us to record and analyse behaviour objectively, we are continually gaining subjective impressions of individuals, which make us feel one way or another about them.

Family history: 1973–1988

1973–1975   During the early years of the project, I was based in Nairobi and worked part time on the study. I first met the EBs in August 1973. On that visit I and a colleague, Harvey Croze, photographed several elephants, including a female that had bony shoulders and carried her head low. In November of that year we photographed this 'head-low' female again with an older female who had two U-shaped tears out of her right ear. I saw these two females together several more times over the next months. They appeared to belong to a small family consisting of about seven members.

In April 1974 Harvey and I decided to put radio-collars on three adult females to determine their movements and distribution. We started searching for a group in the east, in the Longinye swamp, and the first one we came upon was the family with the 'head-low' and 'U-nicks right' females. We chose the older, 'U-nicks right' female, the matriarch, and the veterinarian shot her with a dart containing an immobilising drug. The collar was quickly secured, some measurements taken, and then she was given an antidote. Within a few minutes she was up on her feet and in less than half an hour she was back with her family. We were fascinated to see that the family, although very frightened, would not leave the scene but watched nervously from about 200 metres (650 feet) away. On this day we were able to get a good look at the family and note down the age structure. There were two adult females, two adolescents – a male and female, and three calves – one about two years old, another about five years old, and the third about six years old. Because we often saw them with a family that we had already assigned the code EA to, we gave these elephants the code EB. We named the matriarch 'Echo' because of the sounds her radio collar was making, and called the 'head-low' female Emily.

The radio-tracking proved to be very interesting. Two of the three collared females moved in and out of the park according to the seasons. Echo turned out to be a real homebody. Even when there was heavy rain and the park was deserted by most of the elephants, Echo and her family could be found in Longinye swamp or the Ol Tukai Orok

Above and right:

*Echo, with her long, curved tusks, is
very distinctive and very beautiful.
She is also exceptionally gentle and
non-aggressive, but at the same time
a wise and experienced leader who
has skilfully guided her family
for at least 19 years.*

26

woodlands right in the centre of the park. This sedentary strategy may have been a wise one at that time. During the 1970s there was an unusual period of moderately heavy poaching of the elephants when they ventured out of the park. The other two females were killed; Echo is alive today.

By the time I set up a permanent camp in the park in 1975 I knew the EBs fairly well. During that year the adolescent male departed, leaving six members in the family. By calculating shoulder heights and tusk development together with watching their behaviour, I estimated the ages of the members and worked out the family structure:

Echo	Adult female (about 30 years old)
Erin	Female calf (6 years old)
Emily	Adult female (about 25 years old)
Eudora	Female calf (3 years old)
Little Male	Male calf (7 years old)
Ella	Adolescent female (10 years old)

I could only speculate on the relationship between Echo, Emily and Ella. Ella could be Echo's daughter but probably not Emily's, since calves are generally born four to five years apart. Alternatively, all three could be the daughters of a much older female who had died.

The following is a summary of the major events in the EBs' lives up to 1988.

1976   Environmental conditions can vary markedly from year to year in Amboseli and can have profound effects on the elephants. During this year there was a severe drought in Amboseli and half the calves born to the Amboseli elephants died. Both Echo and Emily had calves but only Echo's son, Eamon, survived.

1977–80   There was higher than average rainfall during this period and at the same time the poaching ceased, making these years very good ones for the Amboseli elephants. Many females came into oestrus and conceived in 1977, creating a baby boom in 1978–79.

One of the first to conceive was 12-year-old Ella, who had just reached sexual maturity. Her first calf, Eric, was born in December 1978. Emily had a male calf, Emo, in 1980, increasing the family size to nine.

1981–83   Rainfall continued to be good or at least average during these years and more calves were born. In 1982 Echo had a female calf, Enid, Ella had a male calf, Ewan, and Echo's daughter Erin gave birth to her first calf, Edwina, at the age of 13. By 1983 Little Male had become independent and was no longer counted as a family member. In October 1983, Emily gave birth to a female calf.

1984   A combination of severe drought and a spate of Maasai spearings caused major losses among Amboseli's elephants, with as many as five deaths in some families. Emily's 1983 calf died in July, but, otherwise, the EBs did remarkably well.

1985   Fortunately the drought ended and the elephants quickly recovered. However, mysteriously in April Echo's son, Eamon, disappeared, possibly speared by a Maasai warrior.

On average the females in Amboseli give birth once every four to five years. Some produce a new calf after as little as three years, some after as long as nine years. Erin gave birth to Eleanor only two years and seven months after Edwina was born – the shortest interval in our records. Echo was not far behind her, producing another daughter, Eliot, in April when her older calf, Enid, was only three years and three months old.

1986–88   The EBs suffered neither droughts nor losses during these years, and Ella and the prolific Erin had young. In addition, Eudora gave birth to her first calf, Elspeth, at the relatively late age of 16 years. Therefore by the end of 1988, the family was flourishing with 15 members.

Family history: 1989

Ninety eighty-nine started out well, with Emily giving birth to a male calf, Edo, in March. Then six months later an event occurred that would have profound repercussions in the family. On 8 September, Emily was reported missing yet Edo and his older brother, Emo, were still with the family. This situation almost certainly meant that Emily was injured or dead. My colleague, Joyce Poole, searched for Emily by car and by 'plane, and eventually found her carcass cloaked by a mass of vultures.

An examination showed that Emily had died not from a bullet or a spear but through human carelessness. There are lodges in Amboseli, and the people who run them do not always dispose of their refuse properly. Both elephants and monkeys are sometimes lured into the unfenced rubbish pits by food left lying around. One of the pits is near the EBs' main route to and from Longinye swamp. Emily's carcass was found less than 100 metres (330 feet) away from this pit. Her stomach contained bottle tops, glass, plastic, used batteries, and many other dangerous items, any one of which could have perforated her intestines. It was a terrible way to die.

Emily's death was the greatest trauma in this family's life since I had met them in 1973. The deaths of calves are no doubt distressing for their mothers, but the death of an adult female disrupts the whole family. As the second oldest female in the family, Emily was Echo's closest ally. She was also mother to Eudora, Emo and Edo, grandmother to Elspeth and a valuable 'teacher' for all the younger members of the family.

The most acutely affected member was, of course, Edo. The youngest orphan to have survived in Amboseli was 26 months old. At only six months old, Edo was eating some vegetation but he was still dependent on milk. He tried to suckle from his sister, Eudora, but she rejected him with persistence and force. Over the next two weeks he got thinner and thinner until all his bones stuck out and he became weak and lethargic. At this point, Joyce contacted Kenya's Wildlife Conservation and Management Department, which sent a team to capture Edo and take him to an elephant orphanage in Nairobi. After several

Sitting in my blue Land Rover, I am accepted by the elephants in
Amboseli as part of their environment. Since 1972
my colleagues and I have followed the histories of the individual
elephants, recording the major events in their lives.

weeks Edo recovered, physically at least. As I write this, he is in Tsavo National Park
with other calves, most of which were orphaned by poachers. Eventually, they will be
released into the wild.

In September 1989 when Edo was orphaned, I was in Nairobi where I was spending
more and more time trying to draw the world's attention to the plight of the elephant.
Poaching for ivory was putting the survival of all Africa's elephants in jeopardy. In October,
I went to Switzerland to attend the Convention on International Trade in Endangered
Species (CITES) conference at which, after a bitter battle, all international trade in ivory
was banned. However, I knew the ban was not enough, that the only way to stop poaching
was to reduce the demand for ivory, which meant increasing the public's knowledge of
and concern for elephants. With this public awareness in mind, I travelled on to Britain

The EB Family

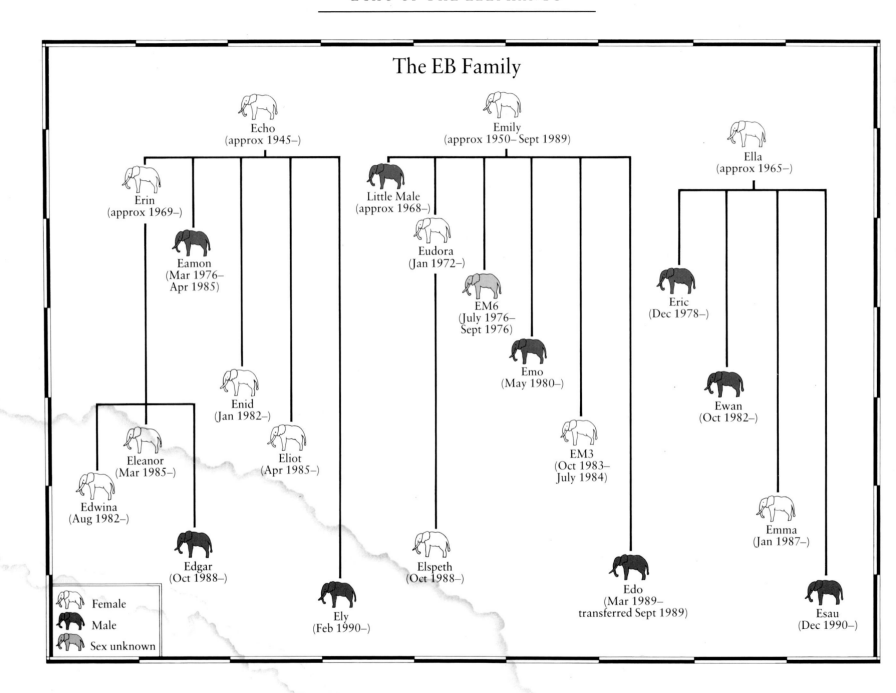

Echo
(approx 1945–)

Emily
(approx 1950– Sept 1989)

Ella
(approx 1965–)

Erin
(approx 1969–)

Little Male
(approx 1968–)

Eamon
(Mar 1976–
Apr 1985)

Eudora
(Jan 1972–)

Eric
(Dec 1978–)

EM6
(July 1976–
Sept 1976)

Emo
(May 1980–)

Ewan
(Oct 1982–)

Enid
(Jan 1982–)

Eliot
(Apr 1985–)

Eleanor
(Mar 1985–)

Edwina
(Aug 1982–)

EM3
(Oct 1983–
July 1984)

Emma
(Jan 1987–)

Edgar
(Oct 1988–)

Elspeth
(Oct 1988–)

Edo
(Mar 1989–
transferred Sept 1989)

Esau
(Dec 1990–)

Ely
(Feb 1990–)

Female
Male
Sex unknown

to discuss with the BBC plans for making a film about the daily life of a family of elephants in Amboseli.

At the BBC I met with producer Marion Zunz and cameraman Martyn Colbeck. I had known Marion for eight years and had great respect for her work. She had always been keen to do an elephant behaviour film with me and we had talked about it over the years. Then Marion and Martyn came to Amboseli in February 1989 to film the elephant sequences for David Attenborough's *The Trials of Life*. We worked well together as a team, and I felt that finally it was the right time and the right combination of people to do a full-length documentary on the elephants. We agreed to begin in January 1990.

On my return to Amboseli in late November, I quickly went in search of the film's prospective 'stars'. I located the EBs as they were crossing an open pan with Echo in the lead followed by her daughters, granddaughters, grandsons, nieces and nephews. It was sad not to see the 'head-low' Emily among them and I wondered how they would fare without her, particularly her daughter, son and granddaughter, Eudora, Emo and Elspeth. On this occasion, Eudora was in the main part of the group with one-year-old Elspeth, but Emo was trailing behind. Even when the family halted, he stayed 15 metres (50 feet) away, seeming hesitant to join them.

Sometimes when the mother of a young adult female dies that female and her calves become less integrated in the family and spend more and more time away from it. When the crunch comes, such as a drought, these are the members who lose out in the competition for the sparse resources. A female as young as Eudora would probably not do well on her own and the chances of Elspeth making it to adulthood would be greatly reduced. I would be watching to see what would happen to them over the next months. In the meantime, though, the EBs still appeared to be a tightly bonded family. Echo was a wise, old matriarch and I thought she would hold them together. As always I felt caught up in their lives and was greatly looking forward to spending the next 18 months with them.

BETWEEN THE RAINS

January to early March 1990

January

Over much of Africa, it tends to rain during certain months, known as wet seasons, and for the rest of the year little or no rain falls. In Amboseli, there are two wet seasons and two dry seasons each year. A long wet season, the 'long rains', extends from mid-March to early June. From mid-June through to mid-October is the long dry season. Late October to early December is the short wet season or 'short rains'. Between these and the long rains is a short dry season, although scattered rain does sometimes fall from December to March.

The beginning of this short dry season was also the start of a new decade. I felt more optimistic than I did at the beginning of 1989 when African elephants were being poached at a terrible rate. Now there was an ivory ban, and I could relax my campaigning work and spend more time in Amboseli. I was particularly looking forward to observing a single family for long periods of time. I had, of course, spent thousands of hours watching elephants, but in a scientific study one must gather data on many elephants before drawing

*In typical EB-fashion, Eliot gazes calmly at
the observer while Emma and Eudora stand unconcerned
less than two metres from the vehicle.
Their trust was the key to being able to enter
and follow the lives of this family.*

conclusions. Concentrating on a small number of individuals would be a new experience which, I felt sure, would give me new insights into the lives of elephants.

In January, Marion Zunz the BBC producer and Martyn Colbeck, the cameraman arrived in Kenya, and on the morning of 16 January we set off from Nairobi, reaching Amboseli in the afternoon. The park was at its best, green and lush after the rains of November and December. Typically of January, there was not a cloud to be seen and Kilimanjaro was visible in all its glory, looking close enough to touch. As we drove across the Serena plain to reach the road to my camp, we came upon a magnificent aggregation of over 200 elephants. More than a dozen families and several adult bulls moved as one, marching slowly towards the mountain in the slanting, late afternoon sun. The whole range of elephant sizes was represented: tiny newborn calves having to run to keep up; playful half-grown male calves stopping to have a sparring match with a companion; newly independent young males forming a little subgroup of their own; adolescent females keeping a careful watch over the young calves; stately matriarchs leading the families; and five large bulls at the rear. I spotted the EBs towards the back of the group but, since it was nearly dark, I decided to introduce them another day and headed for camp.

The camp, which I had set up in September 1975, had recently been moved and rebuilt due to flooding of the original site. It was a comfortable haven hidden away in a glade amongst the palms and acacia trees of the Ol Tukai Orok woodlands. It consisted of seven tents with protective thatched roofs and a kitchen made of offcuts. I had a staff of four: two research assistants, Norah Njiraini and Soila Sayialel, who carried out the day-to-day monitoring of the elephants and lived in a small house at the park centre; and my camp manager and cook, Peter Ngandi, and his assistant, Wambua Kativa, who both stayed in the camp. Also living with us at the camp was a Kenyan Ph.D. student, Kadzo Kangwana, who was studying the relationship between the Maasai and the elephants. Each of us had a separate tent where we slept and worked, and there was a large central dining tent where we met for meals.

It was not until two days later, on the morning of 18 January, that we found the EBs again, this time in the woodlands not far from the camp. I pointed out the adult females, Echo, Ella, Erin and Eudora, and we watched as the family walked about and fed on the palms. They looked superb and Marion and Martyn agreed that they were just what we wanted for the film – a relaxed elephant family going about their normal activities, unperturbed by our presence.

After lunch at the camp, we went back out to spend the afternoon with the EBs. They were moving slowly south on the western edge of the Ol Tukai Orok woodlands and nearby was another family, the OBs, led by Omega. Her one-year-old male calf broke off from his family to come over to the EBs for a play session. The EB yearlings enthusiastically sparred and trunk-wrestled with him, and they got so carried away with their games that the OB calf did not notice he was being left behind by his family. Suddenly he panicked and, head up, ears out, he screamed the deep 'lost baby' cry. Some of the younger females in the OBs came back for him and he ran at full speed across the open pan towards them, looking like a wind-up toy. On meeting, the females reached their trunks to him and he gave a deep rasping rumble. This typical elephant encounter is always wonderful to watch and Martyn and Marion were delighted.

A few minutes later, a car going by sent a third elephant family running into the palms. The Amboseli elephants are not usually frightened of vehicles, but this one must have contained Maasai whose presence almost always alarms the animals. The fear that these elephants exhibited was communicated to the EBs and OBs, and they too turned and walked rapidly back into the palms. We followed them in and found that the third family was the EAs, a group often associated with the EBs. The members of the two families

Overleaf: *The Amboseli elephants live in a multi-tiered social system with the family unit at the core radiating out to bond groups, clans, subpopulations, and the whole polulation including adult bulls. This complex system is highlighted when elephants form large herds.*

were milling together and greeting each other with earflaps, rumbles and the reaching of trunks to each other's mouths.

The relationships between families are complex. Most of the families in Amboseli have special affiliations with one to four other family units, forming what I have designated 'bond groups'. Families in the same bond group greet each other, show friendly behaviour towards one another, and spend more time with each other than with other family units in the population. In addition, certain families share the same dry season home range in an amicable way. I call this level of social organisation the 'clan'. The clan areas overlap extensively and are not held in a strictly territorial way.

There are also two subpopulations, a central and a peripheral one. Aggression among families usually occurs between those from different clans and, particularly, between those from different subpopulations. Many factors seem to determine which families are dominant and which subordinate. The size of the family and the age of the matriarch appear to play important roles, as does the character of the matriarch.

The EBs and EAs belong to the same bond group and are members of the Ol Tukai Orok clan, which is part of the central subpopulation. Echo is an exceptionally gentle, non-aggressive elephant and many, but not all, of the other elephants in Amboseli can dominate her and her family. Within the family she rarely, if ever, pushes her weight and age advantage. In all the many hours I have spent with the EBs, my overwhelming impression is that they are extremely cooperative with each other.

The EBs are also a very vocal and passionate family. They frequently call to one another and if some of the family wander off, even for only half an hour, they will greet each other on their return. Some of the most emotionally charged greetings I have ever witnessed have been between members of the EB family. For example, a few years ago, Emily and her two calves, Eudora and Emo, were separated from the family for about a week. I saw them several days in a row in Ol Tukai Orok without the rest of the EBs. Then one morning I noticed Emily and her calves walking across the open Serena plain that separates the woodlands from the Enkongo Narok swamp. Emily kept stopping and rumbling deeply, and then holding still and listening. Suddenly she gave a different louder vocalisation and this time I could hear an answering rumble over by the swamp. Emily and her two calves started walking rapidly, and I overtook her and parked between her and the other EBs, who were just emerging from the swamp. The three animals were by then running at full speed and the temporal glands on each side of their heads, midway between the eye and ear, were streaming. They raced past my vehicle and joined the others in a wonderful display. Emily pushed through the younger animals and went straight to Echo. The two of them raised their heads in the air, clicked their tusks together, entwined their trunks and roared, rumbled and trumpeted while raising and flapping their ears, and spinning and turning, defecating and urinating. All the others joined in as well making an incredible amount of noise with their loud, almost liquid greeting rumbles. The earflapping, turning and backing towards one another, reaching of trunks to each other's mouths and temporal glands, rumbling and trumpeting went on for ten minutes. Remembering that incident made me think about Emily's death and what the loss meant to Echo, who had obviously had very strong bonds with her.

The following day after saying goodbye to Marion, who was returning to the UK, Martyn and I found the EBs almost immediately. They were feeding on the Serena plain, not far from where we had left them the night before. About 250 metres (270 yards) away, a group of over 100 elephants was coming through the narrow strip of *Acacia tortilis* trees that borders the edge of the open plain. While the EBs were grey in colour, due both to their natural skin shade and the light Amboseli soils, the elephants in the large aggregation were a beautiful red-brown. Their hue gave away their movements over the last 24 hours: they had been in an area of red soils to the south towards Kilimanjaro. Several large males accompanied the herd and, detecting a certain amount of agitation, I suspected there was a female in oestrus (the time when a female is receptive to males and in most cases ovulating). The herd went by into the mixed palm and yellow fever tree woodlands of Ol Tukai Orok.

In the meantime the 14 EBs moved to their own rhythm, which was typical of them.

Above: *The Research Project is based in a tented camp in a part of Amboseli called Ol Tukai Orok, a Maasai name meaning 'Place of the Dark Palms'.*
Below: *Elephants are individually identified by means of tears, holes, marks and vein patterns in their ears. Ella's right ear is easily recognisable.*

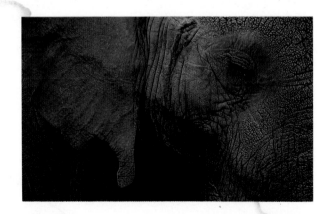

*When family members have been separated and meet again they
invariably greet one another: Eudora (on the left) exhibits
the typical greeting posture of head held high and ears spread
as she backs in towards her family while vocalising,
urinating and secreting from her temporal glands.*

Echo very rarely joined the big herds, preferring to lead her family along an independent path. At 45 years old, 20 years older than the next oldest female in her family, Echo was very much the matriarch. All the other members were aware of where she was and what she was doing. If they were resting and she woke up and moved off, they would move off. If there was a smell or sound of danger, they would look at her first and then act. If she called them with a low rumbling vocalisation they would come, and if she made the 'let's go' rumble they would follow. She was their core, their anchor, their leader.

Today they were feeding and moving, spread out in a loose but coordinated grouping. Each member was clearly visible, providing me with a good opportunity to start learning how to recognise them as individuals. I could already identify them when they were arranged before me like this. However, in order to tell the story of the EBs over the next year or so, I would have to become so familiar with each individual, including all the calves, that I could name them at a moment's notice under any circumstances.

An elephant's ears are its most reliable features for recognition purposes. By the time they are in their teens and twenties, many elephants have outstanding tears and holes in their ears. I am not sure how they acquire the injuries, but it is probably through catching their ears on thorns. Some elephants have much more ragged ears than others, presumably because they have thinner skin that tears more easily. Elephants with very smooth ears can be identified using photographs of the unique vein patterns on their ears. However, the veins are difficult to memorise and, anyway, might not always be visible. In these cases, additional distinguishing features and each animal's overall shape, posture, head carriage and gestures can be used.

I already knew the adult females well. Echo with her long curving tusks and U-nicks in her ears, and Ella with a big chunk out of the bottom of each ear were unmistakable. Erin and Eudora were less distinctive, but still readily identifiable. Echo's daughter, Erin, was remarkably similar to her mother in head and tusk shape, but had very smooth ears with no holes or nicks. Eudora had her mother Emily's narrow head and thin tusks, and she had a few small nicks in her left ear and a tiny hole in her right ear.

Of the three young males in the family, Eric, Ewan and Emo, Eric was the easiest to recognise. His ears were incredibly ragged, forming memorable patterns, and he had a short compact body. Ewan was no problem if seen head on or from his right side, because the top of his right ear folded forwards instead of backwards. When the EBs were all feeding up to their ears in the deep Amboseli swamps, it was often Ewan who gave them away with his folded ear showing just above the sedges. Emo was by far the most difficult of the larger animals to recognise away from the context of the family. Like his older brother Little Male, who had become independent several years before, Emo was the quintessential young male. He had very symmetrical tusks and hopelessly smooth ears, except for one tiny hole in the right ear, which could only be seen under the best of circumstances. But he did carry his head in a remarkably similar way to Emily and Eudora and, with practice, I thought I would soon be able to recognise him easily in any context.

Just as difficult as Emo were the five juvenile females. The youngest was Ella's three-year-old daughter, Emma. Then there were Echo's two daughters, seven-year-old Enid and four-year-old Eliot, and Erin's daughters Edwina and Eleanor who, confusingly, were also seven and four years old. Emma was the easiest because she was much smaller than the others with tusks about 7.5 centimetres (3 inches) long. I also noted that she had a small nick out of the top of her right ear. After her, the most distinctive juvenile was Enid who had splayed tusks which were longer than those of the other calves, and a small U-nick in the middle of her left ear. I recognised the other three calves by their foreheads, a feature I had never used before. Eliot was a veritable prunehead with many wrinkles, Eleanor had only two wrinkles across her head, and Edwina's forehead was perfectly smooth. Edwina also had a convenient bump behind her right shoulder.

The final two animals in the family were the babies, Elspeth and Edgar. They were just over a year old and looked exactly alike except that they were male and female. Fortunately calves of that age stick close to their mothers most of the time. It was only when they went off to play that they could be confused. Then I had to check on their sex, a method which got particularly tricky in tall grass.

As I was studying them, the family slowly wandered across the plain until they reached the edge of the Enkongo Narok swamp. In this area of the swamp there was a large pool of water covered in lily pads but free of thick reeds and papyrus. The elephants drank there and splashed themselves with mud. Afterwards, most of the family went on along the edge of the swamp but two of the young males could not resist the pool. Eric and Emo carefully lowered themselves down the bank and, like people painfully inching their way down a ladder into a swimming pool, they moved gingerly, one step at a time, into deeper water. When the water was halfway up their sides they started sparring and pushing

*Eric becomes a 'monster of the deep' as he plays in the elephants' swimming pool
with his cousin Emo. Young males of Eric and Emo's ages (12 and 10) spend their spare time
testing each other's strength and practising the skills they will need as adult bulls.*

each other. Eventually they fell or rolled over and submerged completely, coming up wearing ridiculous hats made up of the floating vegetation. Soon after, Edwina joined them and the three youngsters played for nearly an hour in the deep water. They pushed, shoved and climbed on one another, ran through the water smacking the surface with their trunks, stood in one spot kicking a front or hind leg violently backwards and forwards making huge splashes, and frequently sank completely with just the tips of their trunks showing above the water.

On the following day, 20 January, we had to spend a few hours tracking down the EBs. They are a relatively predictable group but the core area of their home range is still fairly large, at least 50 square kilometres (20 square miles). We finally found them at 10:15 in a big patch of elephant grass (*Sporobolus consimilis*) to the south of the Serena Road. They were with four other families, but soon Echo broke off from them and headed towards her favourite area, the Ol Tukai Orok woodlands. With the EBs went an adult male, 19-year-old Tolstoy, who had been born into the TD family and was now independent. I noted with interest that Tolstoy was bigger than the largest adult females. Males grow very fast during their teen years and continue growing throughout their lives. Females, on the other hand, grow more slowly in their teens and their growth nearly stops by the time they are 25. At that age, Tolstoy would be towering over the cows and in his 50s he might stand about 3.5 metres (11–12 feet) at the shoulder, while the biggest females would only reach 2.5 metres (8–9 feet).

As well as differing in size, adult males and females also live markedly different social lives. Females are rarely if ever alone, spending their whole lives surrounded by close relatives. The kin relationships among the females in a family are: mother and daughter, grandmother and granddaughter, sisters, aunt and niece, and cousins. They express their attachments by frequent touching of one another and by calling to one another with a wide range of vocalisations. There is a dominance hierarchy based on age, but more obvious is the cooperative behaviour such as mutual defence and the care of calves by members of the family other than their mothers, particularly adolescent females.

In contrast, adult males live a fairly solitary existence. When a male leaves his family he will join other young males or older males or tag along with other families. While he is still in his teens he may need the leadership of the females and therefore will often associate with aggregations of families.

Although a teenage male is sexually mature, he has to go through a long period of growth and social development before he has a chance to mate with females. During his twenties a male begins to spend less time with the female groups and more time with males in 'bull areas'. From 25 years old, males may start to come into 'musth', an Urdu word meaning intoxicated. It is the phase of heightened sexual activity and aggression in a male elephant's sexual cycle. Once a male is over 30 years old, the cycle becomes more clearly defined and by 40, it will be fairly predictable, with eight or nine months of 'retirement' and three or four months of musth activity. In Amboseli, the males over 40 are the ones most likely to mate with females, and the older a male is the more successful he is.

The oldest bulls in Amboseli are in their 50s, and all but one of these is sexually active, and he may be an anomaly. We do not yet know when or if a bull ever retires from competition. It would also be interesting to know whether males ever return to their natal families to mate with close relatives. Answering such questions is one of the reasons I would like to keep the Amboseli study going for at least another 20 years.

At midday I had cause to think more about the divergent lives of males and females. All but two of the EBs were resting in the shade of a fever tree, along with Tolstoy who was right in the middle of the family. The two exceptions were 11-year-old Eric, who was about 2 metres (6.5 feet) from the nearest family member and standing out in the full sun, and nine-year-old Emo, who was nowhere to be seen. After the group finished its rest, Emo arrived with one of his pals from the EAs, 11-year-old Eugene, who was just beginning to spend time away from his family.

Males start to exhibit signs of independence at around eight to nine years old, when they might spend a day or two away from the family. At the same time, the females become less tolerant of these pubescent males and may occasionally threaten them and give them a poke in the backside. While the immediate reason for the aggression is not clear, the underlying reason is to prevent inbreeding by dispersing the sons before they reach breeding age. The males gradually get the message and move towards self-reliance. When they are spending less than 20 per cent of their time with their natal family, we consider them to be independent. The average age of independence is 14 years but some leave as early as nine and others as late as 18.

The death of their mother can cause males to become independent early and I could see from the dynamics in the EBs that this might happen with Emo. Although Eric was nearer the usual age of independence than Emo, he still often stood close to his mother, Ella, and he seemed relaxed about joining the family and moving with them. Without Emily, Emo had no defender in the family who might protect him for a few extra years. Emo was definitely more wary than Eric, carried his head low and submissively, and tended to keep at least 5 metres (16 feet) away from the adult females.

Families may give unrelated pubescent males a hard time as well. On this day, Emo's friend Eugene approached the family so cautiously that it was almost laughable. He advanced very slowly and carefully, one small step at a time, with his head down and his trunk outstretched in a non-aggressive posture. As soon as a female lifted her head or turned towards him he swiftly backed away. However, in six or seven years' time, he would be as big as Tolstoy and the EBs would have to accept him.

After a few days with the elephants, Martyn and I reviewed the time we had spent with the family, and started discussing the film we would make about them. The content would be largely determined by what happened among the EBs over the next months, but there were some specific events we knew we wished to include. We definitely wanted to film a female in oestrus and to follow the development of a calf from its birth. For this reason I looked up the oestrus records for the EBs.

From the records, it appeared that the only female who might come into oestrus was Eudora, and her sexual history was unusual. She was first seen in oestrus in June 1983

When males leave their families they often join up with
other bulls forming what could be considered as all-male clubs.
These four males are all over 20 years old, but, with
the exception of the bull on the left, they are not yet
old enough to vie for the favours of females.

Opposite: Large adult bulls over 30 spend part of
each year in 'retirement' and part in the pursuit of
females. While in this retirement phase, a bull such as
this one will feed and rest, building up his strength
for the exhausting months of his active phase.

when she was 11 years old. This oestrous period was exceptionally long, nearly two weeks instead of the normal four to six days, and during it she had an exhausting time. Some females learn quickly that if they choose a large, older male as a consort, he will fend off other males and she will be left in comparative peace. Although there were older bulls around, Eudora did not stay close to one of them, and was continuously harassed and chased by younger bulls. Generally females conceive during oestrus and give birth 22 months later with no oestrous activity in between. However, Eudora came into oestrus again at intervals during '84, '85 and '86, which showed that she was not getting pregnant. She finally conceived in December 1986 and gave birth to Elspeth in October 1988. Erin had also had a calf that month, but she had already come into oestrus again and had presumably conceived. I thought that Eudora was likely to come into oestrus at some point during the next two years, but it would be impossible to predict when.

The prospects for a birth among the other EBs were much more promising. The oestrus records showed that Ella would probably have a calf in December 1990 and Erin in June 1991. Even more exciting was that the matriarch might be pregnant. Echo had been mated and consorted by males on 8, 9 and 10 May 1988. If she had conceived then, she would have a calf in only a few weeks' time – late February or early March – and we would be able to observe the calf's development for well over a year.

The next day we went out early before sunrise with heightened anticipation of what we would be seeing and doing. Just as we turned into the Serena Road, the big, red ball of the sun started to come up over the Chyulu hills, a long knobby line of volcanic protrusions 45 kilometres (30 miles) to the east of Amboseli. I loved being out at this time, listening to the birds waking, and watching the sky turn from pink to deep rose to golden until the sun actually came up with all the fierce intensity of Africa.

We found the EBs a few minutes later at 6:45 near the large area of elephant or *consimilis* grass to the south of the road. They were moving slowly west, stopping to rest frequently. I looked at Echo carefully and thought that she did, indeed, appear to be nearing the end of pregnancy. Although teenaged female elephants get noticeably larger and more bulbous during the last six months or so of pregnancy, a large adult female does not conspicuously change in shape during the course of pregnancy. Many of the adult females look huge most of the time. Echo tended to be a bit more svelte than some, but now she had a definite bulge and, although she was not suckling a calf, her breasts were large and full. Eliot, her youngest calf, was almost five years old and seemed to be completely weaned, having not attempted to suckle since we had been with the family. Echo usually led her family from place to place, striding out in the front, but today she was definitely looking tired and slow. It took the EBs two hours of stopping, resting, a bit of feeding and slow walking to cross the plain to the shore of Enkongo Narok swamp, a distance of less than 2 kilometres (1.2 miles). Echo trailed along behind most of the way and the rest of the family kept stopping and waiting for her.

Echo's lugubrious pace did not suppress the spirits of the calves in the family. On the following day, after a bit of searching, we found the EBs in the *consimilis* grass to the north of the Serena Road. While the adults were moving slowly, stopping to rest from time to time, the calves were feeling playful. *Consimilis* grass appears to stimulate play activities in youngsters, possibly because they feel secure in the long grass or enjoy the sound it makes as they crash through it. The EB calves soon left their mothers and went charging off, ears out and up, tails curled over their backs, noses stuck out and the whites of their eyes showing. As they ran they emitted nasal, pulsating, play trumpets. When they reached the nearest tall clump they raced through it with heads down and thrashing from side to side. One calf would suddenly spin around and lift its head in mock fear and charge at an imaginary enemy. Eventually pairs of calves stood face to face, entwining trunks and pushing on one another. At one point Erin's one-year-old calf, Edgar, went off by himself to a bare bit of ground. He found a dry ball of elephant dung and played football with it, kicking it forward.

Soon after the youngsters finished their play session, Echo lifted her trunk, smelling the breeze, and all the others did the same. Then she set off with a purposeful stride and led her family through the edge of the palm woodland and out on to an open grassy area where they began to feed. She seemed to have shed her sluggishness and was acting the matriarch again.

Over the next few days, there were a few rainstorms, which was not unusual for January. Rain tends to stimulate the elephants and when we were with the EBs in Ol Tukai Orok on 24 January they were beginning to show signs of restlessness. On that day Ella and her three calves were missing, but I was not alarmed: if any individual split from the family it would usually be Ella. We had sat with the family for about half an hour when they started making deep, throaty rumbling sounds.

When times are good, which for elephants means they feel safe and have enough to eat, youngsters and even adults delight in play. Here, Edgar races through the tall consimilis *grass attacking imaginary enemies.*

*The peace of Amboseli, where there has been very little
poaching compared to other parts of Africa, makes
it possible to observe elephants going about their
daily activities in an undisturbed environment.*

Elephants have an extensive and varied repertoire of vocalisations, ranging from soft rumbles to ear-splitting trumpets. In our studies in Amboseli, so far we have documented 25 distinct calls each with a different meaning. We think there are more. The most common calls are the various rumbles and all of these have infrasonic components, which are sounds below the range of human hearing. These low-frequency sounds can carry over relatively long distances, possibly as far as 10 kilometres (6 miles).

Elephants appear to keep in touch with each other by using certain rumbles. On this day we could hear the low, smooth contact calls, and the contact answers which were louder and rising at the end. I looked around and way over by the trees along the swamp edge I could see three black, wet elephants coming our way. Ella, Ewan and Emma were already running towards Echo and the rest of the family, who had stopped feeding and started moving towards the three. As they ran, the two subgroups rumbled and trumpeted, and then met in a great scrum of elephant bodies. Echo and Ella raised their heads, clicked their tusks together and entwined their trunks. All the others spun around, reached their trunks to each other's mouths, flapped their ears, and screamed and trumpeted in a classic greeting ceremony.

Greeting ceremonies appear to play an important role in elephant society. I believe they help to maintain and reinforce the bonds between individuals in families and bond groups. Whatever their function, there is no doubt that elephants performing them are experiencing very intense emotions. On this occasion the EBs may have been re-establishing bonds before going on a migration, because the next day we found that the rains had made them even more restless. Echo led her family off to somewhere well out of her dry season home range. For the next two days we drove all over the park but could not find the EBs. We did, however, come across a large aggregation out to the west beyond the Ilmberisheri hills. There was a lot of activity in the herd with at least two females in oestrus being pursued by bulls. We then scoured the western part of the park without success.

On 31 January, we headed out towards Ilmberisheri again and found elephant groups dotted all through the bushed grassland below the hills. One of these groups, made up of about 50 elephants, included all the EBs except Emo. Soon the EBs broke from the others and began walking in a determined manner towards the Enkongo Narok swamp. Once again Echo looked large and tired and trailed behind, but even from that position she was still the leader, determining the activity and direction of the group. When they got closer to the swamp they raised their trunks and, clearly thirsty, almost ran the last 50 metres (160 feet) to the swamp edge. After lifting trunkful after trunkful of water to their mouths, they moved into the swamp and began to feed. They stayed in the swamp for several hours and then, late in the afternoon, joined an aggregation of over 200 elephants. This was unusual for the EBs but it was a loose formation with plenty of space for everyone. A herd that size is always an impressive sight and on this last day of January the light was magical. In the slanting beams every crease in the elephants' skin was detailed and their tusks glowed with a golden sheen.

February and early March

Martyn and I had been following the family for two weeks by now and had worked out a routine. Each day we went out before dawn and attempted to find the EBs and stay with them until late morning. Then we came back to camp for lunch, made notes or had a rest, and went back out at around 15:30 or 16:00, staying with the family until dark. We usually got back to camp between 18:30 and 19:00 for a welcome shower and dinner.

Until the rainstorms, this routine had worked well because we were able to key into Echo's movement patterns. Most of the elephant families followed a fairly predictable pattern during the dry seasons. They moved in towards the Amboseli swamps in the morning, drank and fed there for the day, and then slowly headed out of the basin (the old lake bed) in the evening, to eat and sleep in the bushland and grassland surrounding the park. Echo and her family generally moved south towards the mountain at night and

Eleanor was the first to come upon the bones of Emily,
a family member who died in 1989. Elephants behave
mysteriously around the carcass or skeleton of another
elephant, often stroking and feeling parts of it,
trying to bury it, or carrying off the bones.

came into the Ol Tukai Orok swamps and woodlands in the daytime. However, this was proving to be an unusually wet 'short dry season'.

The extra rain was welcome both to the elephants and to Martyn and me. For the elephants it meant more food, for us it meant beautiful skies and no dust. All the elephants were fat and healthy, and had the energy and time to spend in social interactions. Almost every morning the calves had a long play session, sometimes chasing each other through the *consimilis* grass, other times ending up all in a heap on the ground in an attempt to climb on one another. A favourite game was chasing the hapless wildebeests that passed by. Two or three calves would go charging off, heads up, ears out, trumpeting shrilly, and the wildebeests would scatter in all directions.

The rains also meant that the elephants were more likely to wander out of their dry season home range. On 2 February we searched for the EBs throughout their normal haunts with no luck. Thinking that they had probably migrated again, we drove out west to the Ilmberisheri hills where we had found them before, and way beyond. Eventually, tired and discouraged, we gave up and returned to camp only to find them there, feeding peacefully in amongst the tents.

Our morning was not wasted, though, for we had come across Emo over to the west. He seemed to have taken a major step in the process of his independence, being over 20 kilometres (12 miles) away from his family. Emo stayed away for over a week, not returning to his family until 10 February. Probably because of my interest in Emo, I noticed several interactions between the adult females and the adolescent males in the EB family over the next few days. Little Ewan, who was only eight years old, got lunged at by Erin on one day and by Echo on the next. On the morning of the 13th, the EBs were resting out on the Serena plain, while Emo was standing alone under a tree 200 metres (650 feet) away. Later, he was moving with the family but keeping a discreet 30 metres (100 feet) away. A couple of hours after we had found them the next day, Emo arrived with a companion, Kyle of the KB family. Ella immediately turned on Kyle and chased him away. A few days later I saw Ella threaten Emo by folding her ears in a horizontal crease, which is a characteristic sign of aggression among elephants. Emo took one look at her and hurriedly moved away. With such events occurring on an almost daily basis, I did not think Emo would stay with the family for much longer.

A few days later we were reminded once again of the effects of Emily's death on the family, this time in a particularly haunting incident. It was late afternoon and we had been following the EBs as they slowly made their way south towards their night feeding and sleeping area. We soon realised that they were going to pass close to Emily's carcass, which now consisted of bare, bleached bones. Although the wind was blowing away from the carcass, the elephants went straight to Emily's remains.

The first to reach the bones was a young female calf, Eleanor, and right behind her were Erin and Edgar. These three animals immediately stopped and cautiously reached their trunks out. They stepped closer and very gently began to touch the remains with the tips of their trunks, first light taps, smelling and feeling, then strokes around and along the larger bones. Eudora and Elspeth, Emily's daughter and granddaughter, pushed through and began to examine the bones, and soon after Echo and her two daughters arrived. All the elephants were now quiet and there was a palpable tension among them. Eudora concentrated on Emily's skull, caressing the smooth cranium and slipping her trunk into the hollows in the skull. Echo was feeling the lower jaw, running her trunk along the teeth – the area used in greeting when elephants place their trunks in each other's mouths. The younger animals were picking up the smaller bones and placing them in their mouths, before dropping them again. The spell was broken when one-year-old Edgar irreverently began tossing ribs in the air. After a few more minutes they all began to move off, some carrying bones with them, either in the trunk or wedged between the trunk and tusk.

I have seen elephants investigating carcasses and bones on many occasions. Several years before I had actually seen the EBs start to bury the carcass of a young female from another family who had died of natural causes. They had started to kick up dirt and sprinkle it on the body, and a few individuals had gone off, broken off palm fronds and brought them back to place on the dead elephant. Unfortunately, the park's rangers came at that point to collect the tusks and chased the EBs away. I was curious to know how thoroughly they would have buried the body – and why.

Elephants seem to have some concept of death, or at least they recognise a carcass or skeleton as that of an elephant. They do not behave in the same way towards the bones of any other animal, except sometimes human remains, particularly those of a human that has been killed by an elephant. But what is going through their heads when they examine bones and carry them off, or when they bury fresh carcasses, remains a mystery. Maybe one day we will be able to gain some understanding of the cognitive processes in the elephant's brain. In the meantime, we can only observe their behaviour and speculate on its significance.

On the day the family found Emily's bones, her son Emo had, as usual, taken a route parallel to the main family and was on a path about 50 metres (160 feet) away. In February 1990, he was still only nine years old, the youngest age in our records at which a male had gone independent, and I was concerned about him. The first few years of independence seem to be a vulnerable period for young males, even those that leave at the more common age of 14. In nearby Tsavo National Park, newly independent males are sometimes killed by lions, and in Amboseli, we think they are more likely to get speared by Maasai warriors.

The following day we found the EBs back at the Enkongo Narok swamp, at the place we now called the 'elephants' swimming pool'. After a bit of hesitation almost the whole family got into the pool, even Ella and Erin. The only ones left on the shore were Echo, and Eudora and her calf Elspeth. The other calves ran through the water, slapped the surface with their trunks, thrashed the water with their tusks and fell over sideways, disappearing completely. Eventually Ella and Erin got into the mood as well, and submerged and rolled over in the water. Then Erin stood with lily pads on her head and back, and started splashing the water with one front leg, turning the area around her into a froth. Seeing adult females abandoning themselves to delight is a pleasure and shows that all is well, for they must be relaxed and nutritionally fit to behave in this way.

I was not surprised that Echo had abstained from frolicking in the water since, by my reckoning, she was over 21 months along in her pregnancy. Eudora's restraint had a less obvious reason, but accorded with her behaviour within the family since her mother Emily had died. I had been watching Eudora closely and found her strategy fascinating and not one I would have predicted. Instead of taking a subservient and peripheral position in the family, Eudora seemed to be trying to strengthen her bonds with Echo. In elephantine fashion, she was ingratiating herself. She stayed fairly close to Echo and every time Echo moved towards her, Eudora greeted her with a raising of her head and ears, and a deep, gurgling greeting rumble. On this one morning I saw her greet Echo more than a dozen times. The other two adult females, Erin and Ella, did not respond as conspicuously to Echo's approach unless they had been separated from her for a while. In turn, Eudora did not greet these two females in the same way, although her relations with them were amicable. A similar type of bonding probably goes on within families whenever an important adult member dies, but it was only through watching the EBs so intensively that I had gained this new insight into elephant behaviour.

I was now sure that Echo was pregnant and would soon give birth. Martyn and I had got so caught up in the anticipation that we were rather like doting grandparents, watching eagerly as Echo got fatter, her breasts fuller and she became slower and more lethargic.

I had concluded in my studies on oestrus and pregnancy that the average gestation period for elephants in Amboseli is 656. The 656th day from Echo's last recorded day of oestrus was 24 February. But, not surprisingly in such a long gestation, there is considerable variation and Echo could have her calf any time from mid-February to mid-March.

As 24 February approached it became more urgent that we find Echo as early as possible every morning. We had little hope of seeing the birth, because I estimate that 99 per cent of all births occur at night. The elephants are so relaxed around us that I think we would have seen dozens of births if they occurred in the daytime but in all the years of the study, my colleagues and I have only seen two births. Martyn and I wanted at least to see Echo's calf taking its first tottery steps and exploring its new world.

*Elspeth climbs onto Edwina, which is a favourite
game of young calves. Older calves often invite these
activities, but sometimes they are genuinely
trying to sleep and find supporting 200 kilos
of baby elephant a bit disturbing.*

We successfully located Echo every day until, on the morning of 24 February, we found ourselves in a dilemma. As we drove out of the camp, we came upon the EA family and saw that one of the females, Elvira, was in oestrus. Since we knew that, among the EBs, only Eudora might come into oestrus over the next year or so, we had decided to film an oestrous female in the same bond group if we were lucky enough to find one. There was Elvira being hotly pursued by bulls, while elsewhere, Echo's newborn calf might await us. So for the next three days we raced out at the crack of dawn, searched for the EB family to check on Echo, and then attempted to find the EAs and follow Elvira for the rest of the day. This was gruelling and not entirely successful, because we lost Elvira on one of the days, but we did manage to see her mating. Fortunately, by 27 February Elvira seemed to be out of oestrus and Echo had not yet given birth. That evening we observed her moving with the EBs along the edge of the palms, looking very tired and very large.

On 28 February we left the camp just as the sun was beginning to rise on a beautiful, clear morning, and headed down the bumpy, dusty road. At the Serena Road turnoff, a cheetah walked nonchalantly down the side of the road with 20-odd minibuses trailing it. We stopped briefly at what I call Mongoose Junction and watched a dwarf mongoose pop out of a hole in a termite mound, look around and then busily start grooming itself. From the junction we could see a group of elephants to the north across the open plain at the edge of Ol Tukai Orok, very close to where we had left the EBs the night before. We drove towards them and I could see that it was, indeed, 'our' family. Echo and her two daughters, Enid and Eliot, were standing to one side, and between Echo and Enid was a small object – the baby had come!

As we approached, the young male Tolstoy came over to Echo and leaned his tusks and trunk on her back, making a nuisance of himself. Echo still had blood on the insides of her hind legs and the birth fluids do sometimes appear to excite males. Echo moved around trying to avoid him, and the calf was hidden amidst all the legs and feet. When I glimpsed it again it was 'kneeling' on its front legs, with its backside facing the car, and I could see that it was a male. I thought the calf was probably two or three hours old, born in the last hours of the night.

We were so busy recording the scene that it was a few moments before I felt the first pangs of anxiety. I checked with Martyn and found that neither of us had seen the calf up on all four feet since we had arrived. Although he was shuffling round a bit, the calf was still 'kneeling' on his carpal joints (the first joints of the front legs, equivalent to our wrists). In the two births we had witnessed on the project, the calves were standing within

15 minutes of being born. I had observed many calves who were only a few hours old and all had been able to get up on to their feet. This calf's joints were covered in dirt and he had clearly been kneeling for some time.

Five minutes passed, during which Tolstoy wandered off and the calf continued on his knees. In turn, Echo and Enid wrapped a trunk around the baby and gently tried to lift him. He was an exceptionally large and robust calf, and very active. He reached up and tried to suckle from Echo or Enid, searching in the wrong areas – back legs, sides, front feet – as all newborn calves seem to do. After another 20 minutes, Eliot started to follow the rest of the family, which had disappeared through the palms heading north. Then she came back, obviously torn between staying with her mother and following the rest of the group. Five minutes later she went, rumbling, trumpeting and running at full speed to the north, leaving Echo, Enid and the baby behind.

The three of them were out on the open pan in the bright, morning sunlight. Scanning the clear views all around, I spotted the placenta glistening red on the ground about 30 metres (100 feet) away and realised that the calf had hardly moved at all. It was then, I think, we fully acknowledged that the calf had never been on his feet and that there was something seriously wrong with him. Soon two tawny eagles also spotted the placenta and dived down to feed. Dozens of vultures descended within minutes and the air was full of hissing and cackling sounds as they fought over the rich afterbirth.

I watched the calf carefully when he lay down on his side or on his brisket. His feet were bent back completely at the carpal joints which seemed fused in place with no flexibility whatsoever. With one exception, he was the biggest newborn I had ever seen, and I wondered if his large size had caused him to be cramped in the womb, forcing his feet to grow that way. I knew he could not survive for long with his legs bent. Even if he could shuffle along, his 'knees' would soon become raw and infected, and before that, he would die of hunger.

I was wrong about the hunger. At 9:00, through what looked like pure willpower, he found Echo's breast and managed to suckle. Newborn calves often have a difficult time

Below and opposite:
*Ely was born with the first joints of his
front legs, the carpal joints, bent back and
totally immobile. Echo and his older sister
Enid tried to lift him to his feet
and encourage him to walk, but he could
only 'kneel' and move short distances
by shuffling along.*

reaching their mother's nipple. They almost have to rear up on their hind legs, especially those calves that are small and have relatively large mothers. Echo's calf was both strong and tall, and by tilting back and stretching way up he could just reach. I was amazed by his success and also appalled. Convinced that he would die, I felt his ability to get nourishment would only prolong the agony for him and Echo.

For the next couple of hours, Echo kept trying all the things a mother elephant does to get a newborn calf up and on its feet. Every time he lay down, she would prod him with her foot and lift him with the aid of her trunk and foot. Sometimes he screamed the hoarse, deep cry of a distressed calf. When he got up in his kneeling position or tried to suckle, Echo would take a few steps away from him, encouraging him to move. He either stayed put or shuffled forward before collapsing again. Enid also tried to help him up and it was fascinating to watch Echo's behaviour towards her. At first she allowed Enid to prod the calf and try to lift him but later she began to push sideways with her tusks, gently moving Enid away from him. There was no aggression in the movement, which was always done carefully and slowly. While they stood over the baby, Enid frequently reached her trunk up to Echo's mouth, appearing to seek reassurance or information.

At 11:00 they were still out on the edge of the pan in the hot sun having moved only about 20 metres (65 feet) since we had arrived. Both Echo and Enid were flapping their ears at a high rate in an attempt to keep cool. They must have been very thirsty, particularly Echo after the efforts of giving birth. Occasionally, Echo would rumble a contact call and then hold still and listen. We could not hear any responses but she seemed to. Just after one of these calls, Enid rumbled and walked about 10 metres (33 feet) away from Echo and the calf, heading in the direction the family had taken. She stood rumbling with her back to Echo but with her head turned, watching her mother and brother. Then Echo once again tried to get the baby to his feet. He screamed, and Enid whirled and came back to him at a full run, and felt and stroked him with her trunk. She went off twice more, but each time came running back when the calf cried out. It was amazing how strong her instinct to care for her brother was.

Half an hour later, Enid walked over to a small waterhole and splashed mud over herself, and again ran back when she heard the calf. Just after noon, Echo got the calf up with some rough prodding and he crawled along behind her. During the next 20 minutes, they managed to move about 15 metres (50 feet) to a small swampy waterhole where both Echo and Enid splashed themselves with mud, getting the calf wet in the process. The calf lay down with his trunk half in the water, emitting a gurgling sound with every breath. Echo dug in the waterhole, waited for water to gather and drank three trunksful. Then she came out of the hole, and the calf got up and managed to suckle for the second time. It was obviously going to take a lot more than the hot sun and a little mudhole to finish off this strong, determined calf. I kept willing his feet to straighten, but they remained as rigidly bent as ever.

After their mudsplash and token drink, the three animals began to rest standing at the edge of the woodlands. Martyn and I left them at 13:30 and went back to the camp for lunch, but I could neither eat nor drink anything. Hours of watching the calf's gallant struggles and the distraught behaviour of his mother and sister had left me completely drained. I went over to see the park warden and reported that a malformed calf had been born. He listened to the facts and decided that no interference was called for.

In general, Kenya has a policy of non-intervention in its national parks. For example, starving lion cubs are not fed, and sick animals, unless they are a highly endangered species such as the black rhino, are not treated. I fully support this policy, believing that we should not meddle with natural populations and natural processes, but it doesn't make it any easier to sit and watch a crippled elephant calf trying to struggle to its feet or the distraught behaviour of its mother and older sister trying to help and encourage it. Taking everything into account, I still felt that I should confer with the Kenya Wildlife Service (KWS) authorities in Nairobi, particularly with a veterinarian. I had to see Richard Leakey, the Director, on another important matter, and I decided to travel to Nairobi the next day, while Martyn stayed in Amboseli to follow events.

At 15:00 Martyn went out with my assistant, Soila, and I joined them later. Echo,

Enid and the calf had moved about 30 metres (100 feet) and were standing near a larger waterhole where Echo had presumably been able to drink properly. The calf was lying down looking weak and exhausted, and we thought that, despite all his striving, he might die very soon. After watching them for a while, I reluctantly returned to the camp to pack. Martyn arrived back before dark, very depressed. He said the calf had slept for most of the afternoon, but had suckled again. Towards late afternoon rain, presaged by the particularly intense heat at midday, had begun to fall. I did not know whether the rain would help or hinder the calf.

The next day, 1 March, Martyn went out early with my other assistant, Norah, and returned just as I had finished packing up the vehicle and was about to leave for Nairobi. He had found the EBs, and the calf was still alive and shuffling along fairly well. Martyn also reported that one of the calf's feet seemed to have the tiniest bit of movement. Although he added that this was probably wishful thinking, the ray of hope stopped me forsaking my principles, and I did not call the KWS vet when I got to Nairobi.

Martyn kept a detailed diary while I was away, and the following are direct quotes or summaries of his notes, starting from the morning of 1 March:

We found Echo, Enid and the calf not far from where we left them last night. The calf was standing but still on his 'knees'. He looked stronger than he had at the end of the previous day. Perhaps he had benefited from the cool night. As we sat and watched in the dull, morning light the calf slowly followed Echo and Enid. He rarely lay down and continually tried to suckle. He seemed to be succeeding at times but it was an extreme effort. The only way he could reach the nipple was to sit down on his backside. In this way he could tilt at a sufficiently steep angle to reach the breast. We could tell when the calf was succeeding by the loud slurping sounds.

On the second day, Ely had some flexibility in his carpal joints
and was better able to reach Echo's breast and suckle, but he was
still hopelessly crippled. Nevertheless, Echo and Enid watched over
him and patiently geared their movements and pace to his.

In the course of the morning other elephants came and went, and inspected Echo and the new calf. Later, the rest of the EB family arrived and performed a highly vocal and exuberant greeting ceremony. They raced over to Echo with their heads up and ears flapping, rumbling and trumpeting and then turning and backing towards her and the calf. Every elephant's temporal glands were streaming with excitement.

After coming back to camp in midmorning to see me off, Martyn and Norah spent the rest of the day with Echo, Enid and the calf. The family had wandered off again, and Echo moved a bit farther into the palms. At the end of the day Martyn wrote:

One scene stays vividly in my mind. The threesome were heading towards us through the picturesque palms of Ol Tukai Orok. As the two older elephants walked, they continually turned to look back at the calf which was shuffling along behind. Every few feet they stopped and waited for him to catch up before moving on. Their progress was very slow, but they did not show any signs of impatience with the calf. It was a poignant sight and highlighted the incredible, caring nature of these animals.

On 3 March, Martyn went out with Norah at first light and after some searching they found Echo, Enid and the calf deep in the palms. They sat and waited until Echo emerged with the calf following on his knees. Martyn then went on to relate:

Enid came last and when they got out into the open, they paused to feed. It was at this point that we first noticed something both unexpected and extraordinary. The calf was kneeling beside Echo when he suddenly started to try and lift himself up on to the soles of his front feet. I had to double check that what I thought I was seeing was actually happening, and sure enough it was. There *was* flexibility in the front joints; the calf *was* trying and partially succeeding in getting up on to his front feet! I was ecstatic, elated and suddenly full of optimism for the calf's survival and well being.

We followed them out to a clearing where they rested for a while, at least Echo and Enid did. The calf proceeded to give us a display of sheer determination and guts. As Echo rested, the calf shuffled forwards towards the breast. He then leaned his body backwards until his two front legs were almost straight. Carefully and ever so slowly he transferred his weight back towards the front

*On the third day, in a tremendous feat of determination and
persistence, Ely stood on all four feet for the first time.
There were some falls and further struggles, but from
that moment on he never looked back.*

end of his body and simultaneously straightened all four legs. He started to stand, but then oops,
down he went on to his 'knees' again. The other elephants remained still as the calf repeated the
whole slow and probably painful procedure. Each time he tried to stand his little legs would shake
with the effort. We were willing him on as he tried again and again. Finally he straightened to his
full height and stood wobbling precariously. He started to take a step forward to reach Echo's
breast, but as soon as he lifted one foot, down he went. Undaunted, he stretched, stood and fell,
over and over again. But what incredible progress since yesterday!

It rained hard in Amboseli on that afternoon and when Martyn and Norah went out the following morning it was wet everywhere and some portions of the roads were flooded. The rainy season had definitely arrived. Martyn recorded:

We found the whole EB family at the north end of Ol Tukai Orok. Of course, the first elephant that we looked for was the calf and sure enough he was there. We quickly realised that he was looking much stronger and incredibly he was *walking!* His legs were supporting his weight and, unlike yesterday, he was actually moving forward and staying on his feet. The carpal joints would threaten to buckle beneath him but he now had the strength to hold himself up and prevent himself crumpling into a kneeling position. As the others rested, the calf stumbled, limped around and suckled. We now wanted him to take in as much nourishment as he could, unlike when he was first born and, with sadness, we wanted him to fail. He even spent some time using his right front foot to play with a log. He appeared to be trying to stretch his foot by flexing it against the log.

Eventually the others started to move off and feed. The calf was better able to keep up with the rest of the family as they fed. It would not be long before the family would have to make no allowances for him. They did not move very far during the morning but, whenever they did, the calf was right there with them.

When Martyn rang me on 3 March, I knew just by the way he said hello that he was going to tell me something wonderful. His news exonerated any guilt I have ever felt for not interfering in a natural population of wild animals.

On 4 March, Martyn phoned again to tell me that the calf was walking well and showed little sign of the limping and stumbling of the day before. He suckled, walked, lay down and got up again like a typical few-days-old calf. Overjoyed, I decided to name the miracle baby. I wanted to call him Easter for his rebirth, but thought it might offend some people. In the end I settled on the first name that had come into my mind when we realised that Echo was going to have a calf: Ely. It was short and simple – and I had used up almost every other 'E' name in my five 'names for babies' books plus a dictionary of saints.

The next day, my meetings completed, I went to the African Wildlife Foundation (AWF) offices to try to find out more about Ely's condition. Gary Tabor, a vet who had recently joined AWF, had never come across the problem but searched his medical books for me. From my description, he decided that Ely had had 'flexure of the pasterns'. Although this condition was known in domestic livestock, including horses, it had never before been observed in an elephant. It is thought to occur when the dam is disproportionally smaller than the sire and the calf is relatively large. So my initial hypothesis was correct: because Ely was exceptionally large, his legs were scrunched up in the last stages of Echo's pregnancy and completely stiff by the time he was born. I also talked to the Director, Mark Stanley Price, who had seen the condition once in an oryx calf in Oman. Interestingly, he too had had to wrestle with his conscience over whether or not to interfere. He did not and that calf, a female, went on to be a very successful breeder in the herd.

Frustratingly, I had to wait until 7 March before I could get on a flight back to Amboseli. As we flew low to land, I could see a small group of elephants in northern Longinye with my Land Rover parked nearby. Norah and Soila, who were at the airstrip to meet me, reported that the EBs had moved over to Longinye the day before, which meant that Ely had walked a good 3 kilometres (nearly 2 miles) at least. Martyn soon joined us and we all went off to see the family. By the time we got there the EBs had gone into the swamp reeds but I could see little Ely ploughing through the mud and water with strength and energy. I felt like cheering for him.

THE RAINY SEASON

March to May 1990

March

In most years the long rains did not get going until well into April, but by early March they had truly come. It was a welcome change. One only needs to live in the drier parts of Africa for a couple of years to become acutely aware of the importance of rain. Not only does it permeate the soils, it permeates the very spirit of the people and animals of Africa.

The rainy season washes everything clean and provides spectacular skies with something different going on in each quarter. From the flat, ancient lake basin of Amboseli there is a panoramic view of the sky. It is often possible to look west and see a brilliant blue sky, to look north and find huge cumulus clouds forming, to look east and watch a slate-grey storm approaching, pierced by the arc of a rainbow, and finally to see the tip of Kilimanjaro rising above whirling clouds to the south.

The rainy season is also a time of well-being because the rains bring up grasses, herbs and shrubs that supply an abundance of food for all the animals. In Amboseli, the coming

---

*Storm clouds build in a spectacular
Amboseli sky: with only 300 mm falling
in the Park each year, rain is
precious and always welcome.*

of the rains heralds a dramatic change in the movement patterns of many of the herbivores. The elephants, buffaloes, zebras, wildebeests and Grant's and Thomson's gazelles are migratory species. In the dry season they concentrate around the Amboseli swamps for both water and food, but as soon as it rains most of these animals leave the basin and move out on to the surrounding higher ground, where the red soils produce more nutritious and palatable vegetation. In the case of the wildebeests and zebras, the departure is often very dramatic. One day the park might be so full of these grazers that it seems almost like a barnyard. The next day, after one night's rain, the park might have emptied with not a wildebeest or zebra in sight.

The elephants used to leave almost as rapidly as other migratory herbivores, but in more recent years they have tended to stay closer to the park. The change occurred in 1977 after the Maasai moved out of the park completely. The elephants rapidly learned where they would meet Maasai and where they would not, and a few spearing incidents each year keep them wary. The elephants still move in and out of the park but much of their feeding outside takes place at night when the Maasai and their cattle are in their *bomas* (thorn enclosures).

Nevertheless, there remain distinct seasonal differences in the daily routines and association patterns of the elephants. In the dry season there is little mingling of the families, each tending to move on its own within its clan range. A family will leave the basin at night, feed and sleep in the bushland to the south or east, and gradually come back to one of the swamps in the daytime. Families may feed near each other for a few hours in the daytime, but in the evening they usually separate again. The bulls, too, generally stay out in their bull areas and only rarely visit the families.

When the rains come, there is usually a lag of at least a week, while the vegetation responds to the rainfall, before the elephants abandon their dry season routines. But from the moment the rains start there is a restlessness among them, revealed by an increase in interactions and vocalisations. Soon families start coming together in larger groups of 40, 50 or 60 animals, including bulls who have joined the cows and calves. These groups might leave their dry season range and move to areas with the best vegetation. There they will probably meet other families from other clans and the other subpopulation. In years of high rainfall, aggregations of over 500 individuals might form.

It is at this season and in these large herds that elephants are at their most social. For the adults it is a time to re-establish bonds, meet old rivals, settle dominance ranks, and find suitable mates. For the youngsters it is an important time of learning through watching the adults, meeting age-mates and testing one another. Observing one of these big herds is rather like watching a continual party. In one section, two families could be performing an exuberant greeting ceremony and in another, calves might be playing in a great heap of wiggling trunks, feet, legs and ears. In the middle of the herd, three pairs of young males might be having vigorous sparring matches. On the edge, several bulls might be chasing a female in oestrus, while nearby, two bulls in musth could be starting a fight.

When I returned to Amboseli on 7 March to find Ely walking well and moving with his family, the elephants had already begun to exhibit their migratory urge. They were gathering and travelling outside their usual ranges, and we knew it would become increasingly difficult to keep track of the EBs and Ely.

The following day we went over to northern Longinye to the place we had seen the EBs the day before, but there were no elephants in sight. We drove across the plains and past a hyena den which, on inspection, showed signs of recent use. Then we went on into an area called Olodo Are (place of red water) by the Maasai, which is to the east of Longinye swamp and well out of the EBs' dry season home range. After a bit of searching we found them just at the edge of Olodo Are in one of my favourite parts of the park. This area consists of a long strip of *Acacia tortilis* woodlands, fronted by a sward of thick green grass interspersed with white-flowered shrubs. Rising behind the trees and forming an amazing backdrop are the dark greens, blues, purples and glittering white of Kilimanjaro.

On this morning, over 200 elephants were dotted about in a loose aggregation, some resting, some feeding, some already moving towards Longinye. Not surprisingly, the family the EBs were standing closest to was their fellow bond group member, the EAs.

*The coming of the rains and the ensuing growth
of new vegetation mean that elephants
have more time and energy for socialising
and play. Above: Two young adults, a male and
a female, gently trunk wrestle.
Right: Three of the youngest EB calves
start to climb on Edwina, who in this
case lay down to initiate the play.*

Soon after we arrived they all began to move towards Longinye. The EBs and EAs started across the open pan with Echo striding out in the lead and Ely hurrying along beside her. He was doing very well, only a little unsteady on his feet. As they got close to the swamp, the ground dropped off and he stumbled on to his knees going down the slope, but he got up immediately and raced on. The elephants were moving fast at that point, possibly because they were thirsty and wanted to drink. The EBs had travelled a long way from northern Longinye the night before, a minimum of 7 kilometres (4.5 miles) and probably

quite a bit farther. Apparently the members of the family were no longer making special allowances for Ely.

When they reached the water they drank, and then some mudsplashed while most began to feed and drift into the marshy terrain of southern Longinye. Since it was impossible to follow them into the swamp, we went back to camp. In the afternoon we returned to the same area to see what the elephants would do next. Under a dark, leaden and very moody looking sky, we found them in a huge, tightly packed aggregation of over 300, moving south in a broad front across the pan into Olodo Are. It was a spectacular sight, with more than 20 families present and numerous bulls. One of the biggest males in the population, the magnificent M22, was closely guarding a young female in oestrus. We could barely see Ely amongst all the pillar-like legs and when we finally got a good view of him, he looked very tired. His legs appeared to be a bit rubbery and he was struggling to keep up.

I wasn't truly worried about Ely. Echo was an experienced mother, who had successfully raised many calves since I had first met her, and I knew that she and the family would not overtax him now. Animals can be divided roughly into two categories of reproducers – those that produce many offspring rapidly in the hope that some will survive and those that give birth to one or two at long intervals and put a great deal of effort into their rearing. Elephants are very slow reproducers, giving birth to one calf or, rarely, two, after a 22-month gestation period. If the calf dies it would be another two years before the mother elephant could give birth again. If the calf lives she will give birth to another in four or five years, and thus will have invested six or seven years in the older calf. Not surprisingly, therefore, a mother elephant is fiercely protective of and dedicated to her calves.

In nature, the more of one's genes that are passed on, the better. Success is assessed by how many offspring an animal raises to maturity and, in addition, how many close relatives are also raised whether they be brothers, sisters, grandchildren, nieces, nephews or even cousins. This unconscious goal is the driving force that determines much of the behaviour we see in elephants and the elephant social system. Family units probably evolved to ensure the successful rearing of calves and for the mutual protection and well-being of groups of closely related individuals.

A large, adult female elephant is a formidable animal, and one might think she could protect her calves from any predators. However, on her own with maybe two vulnerable and dependent calves at heel, she would have a hard time seeing off a pack of hyenas or, when the system was evolving, sabre-toothed tigers and early humans. A group of 10 to 15 elephants, including three or four adults, can present a wall of defence to predators, and the smallest calves can hide behind and beneath the adults. All the females benefit from sharing in this protection, each being less vulnerable and increasing her success, plus that of her sisters, mothers, daughters, and aunts.

As well as defence against predators, the family unit is also an important environment for the nurturing of calves. An elephant takes a long time to mature and in the process requires a great deal of attention and teaching. There is continuing debate about which aspects of an animal's behaviour are innate and which are learned or acquired. Elephants are doubtless born with some instinctive behaviour patterns, but it appears that a great deal of what elephants eventually do as adults has to be learned. We hoped to see something of this learning process, particularly during the first year of a calf's life, by following Ely.

Over the next few days the EBs continued to move in areas where we either lost them or could not follow them. Then on 13 March they returned to their old haunt, the Ol Tukai Orok woodlands, and we were able to sit and watch Ely and record his progress. He was now two weeks old and was keeping up with the family and suckling regularly, but that was really all he was capable of doing. For protection, care and comfort, he was completely dependent on Echo and the other members of the EBs.

On this morning the family moved to a waterhole where the adults and older juveniles drank. Ely stayed close to Echo, frequently reaching his trunk out to smell and touch her. Surrounding both Ely and Echo was a whole gaggle of little juvenile females, each one

*Rain also brings mud: Ely and Enid seem to be
trying to get as dirty as possible, but
their activity has a purpose; mudwallowing
cools the elephant's body and coats it with
a protective layer of natural suntan lotion.*

Echo with her two youngest calves,
Ely and Eliot. In a rare moment while her
older sister is occupied elsewhere, Eliot is
able to 'allomother' her younger brother.
Juvenile females appear to be irresistibly
attracted to small calves.

trying to manoeuvre as close to Ely as possible. His older sister Enid kept the others away, while she held the prime position of standing protectively over him. Juvenile females are irresistibly attracted to small calves and will crowd round a new baby trying to touch it, pull it closer or lift it. The mother may not welcome their ministrations for the first few days and if there is too much frantic activity, she will often chase away all but an older daughter. Eventually, though, most mothers are more than content to allow the young females to take care of the calf.

The tending of infants by individuals that are not the infant's own mother is known as allomothering. In elephant society, the allomothers are immature females ranging in age from about two to eleven years old and they play an important role in the rearing of calves. The allomothers stand over the calves when they are sleeping, go and get them if they wander away, rescue them from getting caught up in a bush or stuck in a swamp, and rush to their aid at the slightest cry. This behaviour allows the mother to feed and rest in peace for much of the time, which is just what a lactating mother needs. It also prepares the young females for the rearing of their own young, and is beneficial to the calves. Our studies in Amboseli have shown that families with many allomothers have a high calf survival rate. At birth, Ely had six potential allomothers – Enid, Edwina, Eliot, Eleanor, Emma and Elspeth – making him a very fortunate calf indeed.

The young females who seemed to be most keen to stand next to Ely were Enid and Edwina, both nearly eight years old, and little Elspeth who at only 17 months old was already beginning to exhibit allomothering behaviour. I found it interesting that Eliot, Ely's five-year-old sister, was not trying to take care of him. Perhaps she knew that she could not compete with her older sister, Enid, or perhaps there was a note of sibling rivalry. She had been Echo's youngest calf until two weeks before and, although she was no longer suckling, she had probably been in a more favoured position before Ely's birth.

Occasionally, serious competition between siblings occurs. A female may suckle a calf right up until the birth of her next one and sometimes an older brother or sister will continue to suckle even after a new calf is born. It is not uncommon to see a newborn suckling from one side of a female and a four- to five-year-old suckling from the other side. The older calf can usually be weaned after a short while but, if the older sibling is tenacious, the younger calf may die. The death of Emily's new calf in 1984 was probably partly due to Emo's continued suckling, aggravated by that year's severe drought. On the other hand, just a few days before I had seen one female in the EA family suckling her two-year-old daughter and her six-year-old son.

On this day I was interested to note that Ella appeared to be practising a kind of elephantine forward planning, whether conscious or not. She was due to give birth in December 1990 and during February she had sometimes refused to suckle three-year-old Emma. Now in March she was trying more persistently to wean her daughter and poor Emma was suffering. As we watched, she moved forward to Ella's breast, reached her trunk out to touch her and Ella immediately put her leg back thereby blocking access to the nipple. Emma screamed the 'suckle protest', a loud, grating cry of distress that a calf makes when its mother refuses to feed it. Ella moved forward, and Emma tried again and again but, despite her screams, Ella would not give in. Then Emma went around to the front of her mother and tried to reach in between her front legs. Ella swung her tusks sideways, hitting Emma on the forehead, and a bloodcurdling scream arose. Neither Ella nor, interestingly, the other members of the family paid her any attention, and Emma backed away and stood sucking the end of her trunk. Five minutes later she was trying again and eventually she succeeded, but it was obvious that she would soon be weaned.

The calves that are most demanding and most difficult to wean are usually the males; not because they are more gluttonous than females, but because they are growing faster

---

*Overleaf: The rains not only herald good times
for the females and calves, but also for
the adult males who join the family groups
and start searching and competing for
receptive females.*

and need more food to maintain that growth. Male and female calves are about the same size at birth. Yet as adults, females reach about 2.5 metres (8–9 feet) at the shoulder and weigh 3 tonnes, while males can grow to over 3.5 metres (12 feet) and weigh 6 tonnes or more. The greater the male's size and strength, the more successful he is likely to be when he eventually has to compete with other males for the favours of the females.

Ely had a good start in life in terms of body size. An average newborn elephant weighs approximately 120 kilograms (260 pounds) and stands about 85 centimetres (33 inches) at the shoulder. At birth, Ely probably weighed nearer 130 kilograms (285 pounds) and stood about 90 centimetres (36 inches) at the shoulder. He had a lot of growing to do but, fortunately, he did not have to share Echo's milk with another calf and nor would he be likely to for at least three years. Like all elephant mothers of young calves, Echo was tolerant and indulgent and let Ely suckle on demand about two times in each hour.

Just after the adults had their drink Ely moved forward along Echo's side, touched her in a signal that indicated he wanted to suckle, and Echo obliged by stopping and stretching one leg forward so that he could find her breast. He greedily reached his mouth up to the nipple and made loud sucking and slurping noises. Echo drooped her head, curled her trunk up on her tusks and rested, the picture of maternal contentment. He drank for over a minute then ducked under her and started on the other breast, his bevy of babysitters rushing round Echo to stay near him. Enid reached her trunk to his mouth and he gave a deep baby call.

When Ely finished his drink he moved away from Echo and found a small stick which he tried to hold in his trunk. A calf will frequently try to grasp with and manoeuvre its trunk, even a very young one like Ely whose trunk resembled a wobbly, out of control rubber hose. He spent a lot of time wiggling the trunk up and down and around in circles, or sticking it in his mouth and sucking on it. Now the two 'fingers' on the tip of the trunk pulled and pushed the stick, until he finally managed to pick it up. He waved it aloft like a baton and, having accomplished that feat, dropped it and wandered away with his allomothers. They went to a muddy patch near the waterhole, where he started to slip and go down. Although he made no sound audible to my ears, Echo immediately came over, reached her trunk around his middle and pulled him out of the mud and back over to where she had been feeding. Apparently she was not ready to hand over babysitting duties yet.

Over the next two weeks we were able to follow the EBs on a regular basis and watch Ely's development. Among the things he was learning was basic motor coordination. He had to follow the family over fairly rough terrain, negotiating the boulder-strewn paths to the south, climbing over logs in the woodlands and swimming in some of the deeper areas of the swamp. He managed all of these activities as well as any calf his age, displaying no sign of his early crippling condition. The only unusual thing about him was that he seemed to be particularly active. Most few-week-old calves lie down and go to sleep whenever they get a chance. However, when the EBs stopped to feed or rest in the shade of a tree, Ely would frequently remain standing, practising his trunk manoeuvres. Possibly his experiences in the first three days of his life had made him wary of lying down.

It was fortunate that Ely had six allomothers because he was a playful, rambunctious calf. All young calves like climbing on each other and, for Ely, any calf that lay down was issuing an irresistible invitation to play. He always made a beeline for it and started to clamber up on its back or head. Usually he would get his front legs up on the other calf and then just sit there with a ridiculous, satisfied expression on his face.

Ely's allomothers aided and abetted him in this game. One morning, we were following the EBs when they stopped near a bare slightly raised bit of ground and the adult females began to rest. They lowered their heads and either trailed their trunks on the ground or draped them over a tusk. The two older males, Eric and Emo, wandered off to a patch of *consimilis* grass where they lay down, each using a clump as a convenient pillow. Three allomothers moved to the mound and first Enid, then Edwina and Eleanor lay down next to each other. However, instead of settling down to sleep, they raised their heads off the ground and dropped them down again, snaked their trunks along the ground and scissored their legs. The younger calves took one look at them and ran over. Edgar scrambled up

Above and below:
*Elephant calves are born with few instinctual
abilities, instead they have to learn most
of the skills they will need. At a few weeks
old, Ely practises motor coordination by
manipulating a stick in his trunk and
climbing over a large log.*

on Eleanor, while both Ely and Elspeth managed to climb on to Edwina. The two underneath then began wriggling and heaving, and the little ones slipped off with the wonderful rasping sound of elephant skin against elephant skin. Not discouraged, they instantly climbed back up and once again, with lots of flailing and squirming, ended up sliding off. Soon the other young females came and joined in until there were eight calves all in a heap on the ground. Throughout, the adults along with Ewan continued to rest peacefully a few metres away.

A few days later the EBs were mixing with other elephants again in a medium-sized aggregation containing several bulls and about 10 families from different clans and

One of the ways a new calf can be aged is by the degree of pinkness behind its ears. This EB calf's bright pink ears indicate that he is less than 10 days old; by two weeks old the pink is gone.

subpopulations. The herd was feeding and moving slowly to the south of the Serena Road. Soon the EAs joined it and the EBs rumbled greetings to them, some members reaching trunks to each other's mouths. Shortly after, I learned that Echo was not as low in the family ranking order as I had thought. In the aggregation was a peripheral family, the WBs, from the western part of the park, and one of the females in the family had a new calf. Much to my surprise, Echo approached the WBs adopting a very aggressive posture with her ears folded. Although the WBs hurriedly moved out of her way, Echo went straight for the new baby, bent down, scooped it up in her tusks and tossed it a metre or so. It landed apparently unhurt, and the WBs crowded and backed around it looking extremely alarmed. Echo then turned and walked back to her family. In the course of the morning other females from the east attacked the WBs, concentrating on the baby which was obviously their vulnerable point. I interpreted this behaviour as the eastern elephants defending their feeding areas against interlopers from the west. It did not seem very effective, since the WBs did not leave, but then they could not travel far with a new-born calf.

The tables were turned on the EBs a few days later when they were in the same area with a larger aggregation. This herd was made up of a different configuration of families, including the FBs, which are another western family but from a central clan. The EBs were quietly resting in a group when the FBs, led by Freda, a notoriously aggressive matriarch, approached them rapidly and threateningly, forcing them to move away. Not content with that show of dominance, Freda and another female went for Ely and kidnapped him! He cried out and began calling as he was pulled and herded away. Enid followed him, staying close, but Echo appeared confused. She circled around and tried to rescue him by approaching from another angle. The FBs, undeterred, took Ely farther away and at one point he got kicked and knocked down. Martyn and I had to remain strictly observers, as always, and so could not intervene. However, we drove closer to see if he was hurt and, unintentionally, changed the dynamics. Echo was able to reach Ely and Enid, and get them away from the dreaded Freda.

Such events are rare and seem to be the result of a combination of both attraction and aggression. I have seen newborn calves kidnapped by young females from other families on several occasions, but in those cases it was probably due to the strong allomothering impulse. On the other hand, the aggression and violence directed by older females towards calves from other clans is probably a means of working out dominance ranks among the families. I have not seen calves seriously injured or killed in these conflicts and, fortunately, Ely was not an exception.

The next day, 23 March, we found the EBs on their own again in an open grassy area to the south. As usual, we sat watching them from my blue Land Rover, trying to be 'flies on the wall', but on this occasion we were thwarted. Now that he was over three weeks old, Ely was doing a lot more exploring. He would go on forays several metres away from Echo, accompanied by various allomothers. I had parked the car about 20 metres (65 feet) from the family but they were feeding and moving slowly towards us. Ever since Ely was born my vehicle had been a familiar part of his environment and, as the elephants got closer, he decided to investigate it. He walked straight up to the front, reached his trunk out and wrapped it around the front 'cow-catcher' guard rail and began pulling. Although he looked small, amazingly he was able to rock the vehicle. His main babysitter, Enid, stood back from the Land Rover and looked slightly agitated, clearly not 'approving of' this activity, but she did not pull him away. After a while he got bored with the game and went back to her. Over the next four days, Ely came over to the vehicle from time to time and felt it, pushed it or rocked it, apparently considering it a fairly good toy.

Having become totally caught up in the EBs' lives for two and a half months, Martyn and I reluctantly had to suspend our observations at the end of March. He had to return to the UK and I had duties to perform that would take me away from Amboseli. We planned to resume filming in June. In the meantime, my assistants, Norah and Soila, would try to keep track of the family while continuing to collect data on all the elephants.

*Ely has a great deal of growing, developing
and learning to do before he becomes a large
bull in his prime, but in the meantime
a romp in the swamp is very satisfying.*

Opposite: *A bull crosses one of Amboseli's
flooded pans at dawn. When a bull is actively
seeking females he spends a considerable
amount of time travelling in and outside
the Park in his search.*

April and May

The rains continued with renewed vigour in April and May, the months of heaviest rainfall, and it became difficult to get around in Amboseli. The old lake basin is the lowest point around and parts of its surface are very hard, and therefore rainwater has a tendency to just sit on the surface. At times it almost appeared to be reverting to a lake. Nevertheless, Norah and Soila braved the flooded roads and muddy terrain to keep us posted.

Typically of the homebody EBs, they did not venture far during the height of the rains, nor did they join the big aggregations very often. Ely was very active, playing vigorously and exploring away from Echo. Ely's main allomother was still Enid who was rarely more than a metre or so away from him.

Towards the end of April I went down to Amboseli to carry out routine administrative tasks and decided to visit the EBs. On 28 April, when Ely was exactly two months old, I drove out into the sodden park between the pools of standing water. I toured the EBs' usual haunts near the Serena plain and Ol Tukai Orok. By good luck I found them on the edge of the woodlands, just as they were entering an area that had turned into a marsh.

I parked next to the edge of the water and began to do a census of the family. As I was ticking off the members, an extraordinary thing happened: Echo turned at right angles to the direction she was moving in and walked straight over to the Land Rover. She stopped so close to my driver's door that I could have reached out and touched her, and stood quietly looking in at me. I talked softly to her because the elephants are familiar with our voices and become more relaxed when they know the people in a vehicle. When I had arrived she and a few others had started secreting from their temporal glands and by the time she reached the car the sides of her face were streaming with tear-like liquid. This behaviour is a sign of social excitement used, for example, during greetings. I could only suppose that our presence nearly every day for two and a half months had made us almost as much a part of her daily routine as she had become of ours. She didn't vocalise or signal in any other way, simply seeming curious and 'friendly'. She then moved to the other side of the car and stood looking in the passenger window.

Ely had gone off with Enid and Elspeth when Echo came over. While all the elephants had put on weight, Ely had grown tremendously in the one month. I watched him as he pushed and shoved Elspeth, trying to initiate a game. Then, several minutes after Echo had turned and moved on in her original direction, Ely suddenly spotted the Land Rover. As soon as he saw it, he left his companions and came straight over. He was a little more cautious than he had been a month ago, reaching his trunk out towards the vehicle from a metre or so away. A few moments later he got up his nerve, came closer and lightly touched the door with the tip of his trunk. When he grew bored and wandered off, I was surprised to see him plucking up blades of grass here and there, and chewing on them. Most calves do not even try to start feeding on vegetation until they are between three and four months old.

This encounter made me look forward even more to the dry season when Martyn and I would once again become a part of the rhythm of the E Bs' lives.

THE DRY SEASON

June to early November 1990

The Early Dry Season: June to late September

By June the rains had ended, but Amboseli was still green, and the vegetation continued to grow, fed on the moisture remaining in the soils. It was the beginning of the cool months in East Africa; in July and August the days are overcast and temperatures rarely reach 80°F (27°C) in the daytime and frequently drop below 50°F (10°C) at night. June is less predictable; some days are hot and sunny, while others are cold and gloomy. The elephants too are unpredictable, not having settled down into their dry season routine.

Martyn and I arrived back in Amboseli late in the afternoon of 12 June to be greeted with the news that there was a dead elephant in an area called Njiri. The next morning we drove there with Norah and Soila, and dozens of vultures led us straight to the body. It was the carcass of an adult male who had been dead for a few days. The once magnificent animal was reduced to rotting flesh and exposed bones and smelled exceedingly unpleasant. The park's rangers had already removed his tusks, which turned out to weigh 13 kilograms (29 pounds) each, indicating that he had been a fairly large bull. I shooed away the vultures

Elephants prefer fresh grass, but in the dry season after the grass has been eaten down they turn to other vegetation. Echo is feeding on a large palm frond while Ely investigates what his mother is doing.

and, trying to hold my breath, photographed his ear for identification and measured his foot to determine his relative size and, thus, his age. An elephant's foot size is correlated with its shoulder height. Since an elephant grows throughout its lifetime the shoulder height is a good indicator of age. We also tried to work out how he had died. Although there were no obvious wounds on the side we could see, I did not think that he had died of natural causes.

Every year a small number of males disappear never to be seen again and there is no evidence to suggest that they emigrate to other areas. Eventually, after a year with no sightings, we have to assume that they are dead. The loss of a female or calf is easier to be certain about because they form part of permanent groupings. If a family member is missing on several sightings and, in the case of an adult, her calves are still there, or, in the case of a calf, her mother is still there, we are fairly sure the animal is dead.

We know that the Maasai spear elephants from time to time as part of their ritual of warriorhood. We also know that some poaching of elephants occurs. Fortunately, the losses have been relatively few since the late 1970s. However, bulls, cows and calves travel freely into other parts of Kenya and across the border into Tanzania, and sometimes individuals fail to return or come back wounded to the park to die. I suspected that the latter fate had befallen this bull and hoped that his death did not indicate an upward trend in poaching or spearing. It made me slightly uneasy about the other elephants, including the EBs, who had not been sighted by Norah and Soila since 30 April.

We had to spend the rest of the day checking in with the warden and organising equipment, and thus it was not until the following day that we set out on our search. We were able to reassure ourselves about the EBs after only an hour of driving round Echo's favourite areas. All 15 members, including Emo, were happily munching palm fronds in the Ol Tukai Orok woodlands. We got a brief glimpse of Ely before he disappeared into the thick palms.

The next morning we set out at dawn hoping to spend a full day with Echo and her family. We searched down the Serena Road and all through the Ol Tukai Orok woodlands but both areas were decidedly empty of elephants. Over in the Longinye swamp there were some elephants, but not the EBs. We then drove round the eastern side of the swamp, ending up back on the north-western side, and crossed over to the other major swamp in Amboseli, Enkongo Narok. There we found some of the western families.

At 11:05 we arrived back at the Serena Road and saw the EBs just coming in from the south. They were moving fast and looking nervous, their red colour showing that they had been out towards Kilimanjaro, possibly into areas where they were vulnerable. The family went into the palm woodland where it was difficult to follow and we decided to leave them. We were tired after four and a half hours of searching, covering a circuit of over 60 kilometres (40 miles). In addition, I had an excruciating headache which I suspected was the beginning of a bout of malaria. On our return to camp I took the appropriate drugs and went to sleep. Martyn went out in the afternoon and stayed with the EBs until dark, when they gradually made their way out to the south in the direction of the mountain.

The next day Martyn had a bad stomach bug. With dead elephants and sick people, our second period of observation seemed to be getting off to an inauspicious start. Nevertheless, on the following day we were both better and left at dawn to find Echo and her family. Once again, we searched in all the areas the EBs tend to use and some they do not, without success. In the evening, we came across them near the elephants' swimming pool, in an area that we had checked at mid-morning. It seemed likely that they had entered the park late again.

In most months, the EBs' daily routine starts at around 4:00 in the morning, when they wake up from their night's sleep. They move slowly into the park towards the swamps or woodlands, sometimes feeding on the way, maybe having a play session shortly after dawn. Their destination for the day is probably determined by Echo before they enter the park. On arrival, they drink at a waterhole and mudsplash or mudwallow, depending on the air temperature. Afterwards they find a spot with loose, dry soil and dust themselves thoroughly, followed by a good scratch against a tree or mound. Feeding and resting, with at least one nap around noon, occupies the rest of the day. At around 17:30 they slowly

In the course of their daily activities elephants dust themselves
frequently: the fine particles of earth reflect the sun's rays
thereby protecting the elephant's nearly hairless skin,
and at the same time provide an abrasive substance
for dislodging ticks.

set off in the direction of their night's destination, again probably determined by Echo. They leave the woodlands or swamps, and may have another play and socialising session before reaching their night feeding area. There, they feed until around midnight, and then all lie down and sleep for three or four hours.

The EBs were obviously departing from this routine and on 18 June, we changed our strategy in an attempt to determine what was happening. Instead of rushing all over the park looking for them, we waited at Mongoose Junction, which is on a rise offering a clear view in all directions. We got there early in the morning prepared to wait until midday. At 7:00, one small group, the TAs, went past. By 9:00 we had had breakfast and were starting to get restless when we made a 360 degree scan with binoculars once more. Out towards the mountain, more than a kilometre beyond the park boundary, we saw a family that looked somehow 'EB-like'. We decided to drive closer, which was not an easy task. We were on the northern edge of lava fields that extend all the way back to Kilimanjaro and provide a gruelling surface for both vehicle and passengers. Beyond a certain point, the boulders are so large and numerous that the fields become impassable.

Weaving and lurching across country, we managed to get within 50 metres (160 feet) of the elephants and saw that they were indeed the EBs, all present and healthy. They were wary when we first arrived, but I spoke and they visibly relaxed on hearing my voice. Around 10:00, a herd of sheep and goats went by with two Maasai herders. The

The EBs turned out to be champion sleepers during the middle of the dry season. Here Eliot shuts out the world with one large ear. (Note the ticks, a large species that only feeds on elephants, lodged between her front legs.)

EBs raised their trunks, smelled the air and started moving away. However, they headed off towards the mountain not towards the safety of the park. They stopped at a small, thorny *Balanites* tree and rested under it, and remained there until we left at midday. When we went back later in the afternoon, we found them moving steadily to the south-east, away from the park.

From their movements, I knew that the EBs were into what I call the 'French holidays'. This exodus from the park tends to occur in July and, particularly, August. It reminded me of August in France, when most businesses and factories close down and everyone goes on holiday at the same time. This year the elephants appeared to be having their 'holidays' a bit early.

The exodus is a hiccup in the otherwise straightforward ranging patterns of the Amboseli elephants. In the wet season, they travel to wherever there is good grazing, whether it is inside or outside the park. They search out the most palatable and nutritious of the grasses which flourish with the rains. In the dry season, as the grasses are eaten down, the elephants retreat to the woodlands and swamps in and around the park. By the late dry season they are almost completely dependent on the swamp vegetation. However, at some point during the long dry season, usually in July and August, the elephants are lured out of the park again, attracted to the *Acacia nubica* bushland at the base of Kilimanjaro. Presumably these small trees are particularly delicious then; perhaps the sap is flowing and there are nutrients in the bark or leaves that the elephants need. In any case, most of the families and bulls spend a great deal of their time feeding on the *Acacia nubica*, both during the day and at night. Since there is no available water out there, they have to come back into the park at least every other day to drink.

The elephants' daily activity pattern also varies according to the season. Generally elephants spend about 16 hours a day feeding, interspersed with time for drinking, mudwallowing, dusting, scratching, socialising, playing and resting. In the wet season, the highly nutritious vegetation available allows them to spend less time feeding and more time socialising. In the dry season they have to work much harder to get enough to eat.

Over the following two weeks, we became familiar with Echo's 'holiday' routine. She took her family out to the mountain in the late evening, and spent that night, the next day, and part of the following night out there. Then in the early hours of the morning they came back into the park to the swamps to drink and rest. Martyn and I observed them on the alternate days that they were in the park.

A typical day during this period was 3 July. We left camp at dawn and saw the TAs crossing the Serena Road heading towards Ol Tukai Orok. There was also one elephant in the *consimilis* grass to the north of the road, which we assumed was a bull. We drove on to Mongoose Junction and scanned in every direction but did not see any more elephants. When we went back to check on the animal in the *consimilis*, we discovered that it was Echo, the only one of the 15 EBs on her feet. The rest of the family were lying down sound asleep, even Ella, Erin and Eudora. Soon Echo too lay down and for about 10 minutes there were no elephants in view, just a few grey humps in the long grass. They stayed there from 7:00 until 10:30, moved about 100 metres (330 feet) and began resting again. Ella lay down right next to the car alongside her calves and made bubbly, snoring sounds through her long trunk. Around noon the family sleepily made their way towards the swamp, arriving at the edge at 12:20, over five hours after we had found them. They waded into the swamp and were soon obscured by vegetation up to their ears. We went back to camp and returned to the swamp edge in early evening to find them still feeding. We waited there until they started heading off just as the sun was setting.

Their behaviour indicated that they did not sleep very much while they were out of the park. Probably they were too busy feeding and keeping track of the Maasai and other humans who might pose a threat. We were always relieved to see them arrive safely back, but that relief soon gave way to boredom. Instead of fascinating glimpses of Ely practising and using new skills, we would see him and the other calves move to the *consimilis* grass without a flicker of playfulness. In less than a minute, the first calf would collapse into a sitting position and flop over on its side. Soon most of the others would slowly subside as well, remaining prone for hours.

On the days that the EBs stayed out towards the mountain, Martyn and I took the opportunity to focus on the lives of the males, particularly their sexual cycle of musth and retirement. Bulls begin coming into musth when they are in their late twenties, but they do not have regular cycles until they are nearing 40. The sexual cycle is a yearly one, at least in Amboseli. Generally the large males over 40 spend three to four months in musth and then eight or nine months of the year in retirement leading a very peaceful, somewhat solitary life.

My colleague Joyce Poole studied the sexual activity cycle of males and found that, when they are not in musth, Amboseli males retire to bull areas, of which there are three. Two of the areas, one to the west and one to the south-east, are on the periphery and outside the park, and are not often used by the females and calves, or only at night. The bulls living in the third area in the centre of the park, tend to feed in the very deep swamps which the family groups do not use. Thus, when a bull is not in musth, he remains more or less segregated from the cows and calves.

In my more frivolous moments I think of the bull areas as all-male clubs. The males in retirement hang out with a few buddies or move about on their own, feeding a lot, and getting plenty of rest so that they build up fat reserves for the three or four busy months of musth ahead. I can sometimes almost picture them sitting around in leather armchairs reading *Wall Street Journals*.

When a bull comes into musth he makes a strikingly different impression. Musth is similar to rutting behaviour in deer, in that males exhibit physiological changes, become aggressive and pursue females. However, in most deer, the does are only receptive for a

The magnificent M22, who is around 50 years old
and the third largest bull in the population,
stretches for a palm frond way out of reach of
even the biggest females.

certain period of the year and all the stags in a region come into rut together at this breeding season. The stags, with their newly grown horns, posture and roar, fight other males, and try to herd and mate with females, all in a matter of weeks. Elephant females tend to come into oestrus during and after the rainy seasons, but the breeding period covers at least eight months, and females can be receptive in any month of the year. Therefore, the bulls' cycles are not synchronised and, at any point in the year, there will be some bulls in musth.

There are 177 adult, independent males in the Amboseli population. Of these, 26 are over 35 years old and are the prime breeding males. At the pinnacle of this group are five huge males: M13 (Iain), M126 (Bad Bull), M22 (Dionysus), M45 (Patrick) and M7 (Masaku). Their musth periods are spaced out from each other so that they are rarely in competition, which helps prevent dangerous conflicts. Bulls in musth have been known to kill an opponent.

The second largest bull in the population, M126, was in musth when the EBs were going off to the mountain. Unfortunately, we could not risk trying to film this male. He was given the name Bad Bull because he is extremely aggressive and feared by all the elephant researchers. He will go as far as 200 metres (650 feet) out of his way to threaten and charge us. We always carry out essential observations of him from a place with a clear escape route and otherwise give him a wide berth.

Just as all the researchers have favourite family groups, we also have favourite bulls. At the top of the list is the third largest male in the population, the magnificent-looking M22. He is about 50 years old, and probably weighs 5–6 tonnes and stands about 3.4 metres (11 feet) at the shoulder. His tusks are very wide at the base and sweep out and down then up again. His popularity stems both from his stateliness and the fact that he is amazingly tolerant when he is in musth. Far from terrorising us, he does not even acknowledge our presence. The only accommodation he makes is to walk around our vehicle rather than through it, displaying even less interest in us than in a bush which at least provides something to eat.

M 22's musth period covers January to early April, which is a very good slot because numerous females come into oestrus during the months following the short rainy season. Earlier in the year Martyn and I had admired M 22's adeptness at finding females at the crucial point in their oestrous cycle when they were most likely to be ovulating. He moved very busily back and forth across the park, guarding and mating with a female in Kitirua in the west on one day, and then appearing beside a different oestrous female in Olodo Are in the east on the next day. It was an impressive display of tracking skill and timing which, I estimated, earned him at least a dozen calves.

Now in his retirement phase, M 22 was living in the bull area in the centre of the park, which meant that we saw him frequently. He wandered about with a slow, purposeful stride, feeding on palms or acacia trees. Being so tall, he was able to reach succulent bits, such as dates and pods, which the cows and calves could not get. In addition, his strength allowed him to pull branches off the large trees. He could strip the bark off even the smallest of them in a feat of coordination that was a pleasure to watch. He would chisel up a piece of thin bark with his tusks. Then, holding one end of the branch with his foot and grabbing the loose bark with the 'fingers' of his trunk tip, he would pull the bark off in one long piece, place it in his mouth and eat it. Sometimes he went off to Enkongo Narok swamp near the swimming pool and disappeared into the dense papyrus in water over 2.5 metres (8 feet) deep. Occasionally he was joined by younger bulls who appeared to be warily attracted to the very large males. If a family group was around, he might feed near it but would not show any interest in the females.

In early July, our days with the males ended. The E Bs started coming into the park

Overleaf: *The large AA family, another favourite of the research team, crosses the pan in a long column on their way to Enkongo Narok swamp. In their daily routine the elephants come into the swamps in the morning and move out into the surrounding bushland in the evenings.*

every day again, and doing things other than sleeping. Even more fortuitous, they were spending all their daytime hours in the area of the Ol Tukai Orok woodlands in and around my camp. There were four or five families in the population that were very habituated to the tents and people in the camp, and would come up to the periphery to feed on the grasses and palms. Two of these families, the TAs led by their matriarch Tuskless, and the EBs, would come right in and feed around the tents and shower, even venturing among the laundry hanging from the lines behind the kitchen. Their fearlessness allowed them to get the last of the good grasses, without having to compete for it with the rest of the population.

Having the elephants right in camp meant that we could observe them from a different perspective from the one we had in the Land Rover. One of the first things I noted was that Ella's breasts had shrivelled to one-quarter of their size when she was lactating. Her daughter Emma, now three years and five months old, did not appear to be attempting to suckle any longer. Therefore, Ella's next calf, due in about six months' time, would not have to compete for its mother's milk.

We were particularly delighted to have excellent views of little Ely. He was four months old, and growing and developing very fast. In late April, when I had first seen him feeding, he could pluck up one or two blades and put them in his mouth but was not feeding on vegetation seriously. On 9 July, when the family was next to my tent, I saw Ely making much more determined efforts to obtain grass, chew it and swallow it. He managed fairly well, although his trunk did not have quite the strength or coordination needed for many of the clumps. As I watched, he twirled his trunk around and around a bunch of grass, got a good grip and then pulled. The grass broke off but fell to the ground and he had to scoop it together with his trunk. He then brought it to his mouth grasped in the 'fingers' on the end of his trunk. The next clump he tackled was bigger and tougher, and would not give. He wrapped his trunk around it tighter and pulled again and again without success. Finally, he 'cheated' and simply knelt down and bit the grass with his teeth.

On this day only 13 of the 15 EBs were present. The missing pair, Eric and Emo, had been sighted by Norah and Soila with Tuskless and the TAs on one day and with the AA family on another. These adventurous young males were exploring new terrain and testing out their social status. While Emo had been coming and going ever since his mother had died, it was the first time we had recorded Eric leaving the family.

A few days later, Martyn and I reluctantly left Amboseli for another couple of months, he to return to the UK and I to go to Nairobi. Again, Norah and Soila kept us in touch with the EBs as well as monitoring the whole population. From them we learned something of Eric and Emo's movements.

On 14 July they saw Ella and her two younger calves with Eric and Emo, but separated from Echo and the others. On 23 July, Ella was reunited with Echo, and Eric and Emo were absent. There were two more sightings of the EBs at the end of July, five during August and one in September. Eric was present every time and Emo on all but two. Emo was spending over 50 per cent of his time with the EBs, indicating that he was not yet ready for independence. Despite his somewhat insecure position as a pubescent male without a mother, he still appeared to need Echo's leadership and the companionship of his relatives.

The Late Dry Season: late September to early November

I returned to Amboseli on my own on 29 September and found a dry and desiccated park. There had been no rain for three months and the famous, powdery alkaline dust of Amboseli had settled over the vegetation bordering the roads, giving everything a dull, dry appearance. The air was hazy with the dust and Kilimanjaro appeared through it as a faint blue-grey outline far in the distance. By midday dozens of dust devils were swirling around the plains. The grass was reduced to a stubble out on the plains and was well cropped down at the edges of the swamps. The grazing animals were concentrated around the park's two major swamps, Longinye and Enkongo Narok, and around the smaller waterholes in Kitirua and Ol Tukai Orok, including the ones near my camp. Wildebeests,

zebras and elephants came into the camp, some feeding boldly on the grass right under the thatched roofs. Two male zebras seemed particularly at home when I arrived. One was an old stallion who had presumably given up the struggle to keep a harem of mares and the other was a young male with a strange spotted pattern who was probably not ready to try to secure females yet. They walked confidently on the paths between the tents, barely getting out of our way when we passed them. The 20 or more wildebeests that entered the camp each day were more nervous. Every time one of us appeared out of a tent, they panicked and went stampeding off, only to return a few minutes later. Tuskless and the TAs arrived nearly every day at noon and rested under

Left and below:
*At the height of the dry season there is little left
to eat except for the vegetation growing in the swamps.
The elephants wade right in up to their ears
and feed in the swamps for hours; however, some
take time out for recreation.*

the tree in the centre of the camp. As long as we did not move fast they paid no attention to the resident humans but they did take notice of strangers. Other elephants fed on the palms and around the small swamps at the periphery of the camp.

In the open glade just to the south a variety of species converged to drink and feed, including warthogs, bushbucks, buffaloes, giraffes, impalas, a rhino or two and our resident pair of lions. At night we could hear the lions roaring, plus the sounds of hippos, baboons, leopards, hyenas and jackals. With so many animals in and around it, the camp resembled a barnyard. Our once-green lawn was dug up and covered in dung, which I was sure would be beneficial in the long run but did not look very attractive.

Having concentrated on the EBs for most of the year, I felt out of touch with the rest of the elephants in the population. Therefore I decided to spend my time until Martyn arrived carrying out censuses on as many families as possible and taking photographs to update the recognition file. On the morning of 30 September, I was setting out to start on these tasks in the east when, right at the entrance to the camp, I came across 12 of the 15 EBs. The three missing members were Ewan, Emo and Eric. The rest of the family were feeding on the huge fronds of the *Phoenix reclinata* palms. These plants never looked very appetising but clearly had some nutritional content. After about 15 minutes, Ewan arrived from a small swamp to the west. When I left them, there was still no sign of Eric and Emo, but they could have been hidden behind the palms.

Over the next week, I had an enjoyable time reacquainting myself with the rest of the elephants. Then Martyn arrived in Amboseli on 15 October and, after a day of preparations, we set out to find the EBs on the 17th. Of course, when we wanted them, they were not at the entrance waiting for us. We searched from 6:30 till 12:30 and started again at 16:30. About half an hour later, we finally spotted the long graceful curves of Echo's tusks emerging from a giant palm at the southern edge of the Ol Tukai Orok woodlands. Soon we recognised Ella with her head stuck deep in another palm, and Erin and Eudora feeding on grass farther back. A closer survey revealed that all the EBs were present except for Emo. As we watched, the family came out of the woodland and started across the open pan. A little later two young males emerged from the palms and these turned out to be Emo and his friend Eugene from the EAs. They crossed on a parallel path, not exactly with the family but not truly on their own either.

That night there was lightning towards the mountain and a smell of rain in the air, and the following morning we woke to see a light coating of snow on Kilimanjaro. It was a lovely and welcome sight, bringing hope of a good wet season. Generally in Amboseli, the short rains do not come until November, but sometimes they start as early as mid-October. The earlier the rains come the better they usually are.

For the next few days, the EBs and the other families that shared their clan area followed a typical late dry season routine, spending the major part of their day feeding in and around the swamps. The EBs usually arrived at the swamp edge or their favourite patches of *consimilis* grass by dawn and did not leave for their night feeding and sleeping area outside the park until after sunset.

By this time of year, food normally became scarce and the elephants showed signs of a poor diet. However, the ones we encountered looked fine. The adults were beginning to look a little bony around the shoulders and pelvis, but they were not unduly thin. Many of the calves, especially the ones that were still suckling, continued to be butterballs, with a quilted pattern produced by fat puffing out the skin between the wrinkles. There was very little play among the calves, though, and all the elephants were moving slowly, presumably to conserve energy.

When the EBs went deep into the Enkongo Narok swamp we could not follow them, but when they went into Ol Tukai Orok we were able to stay with them for most of the day. The 21 October was one of the days that Echo led her family into the woodlands. They slowly moved through the trees, feeding as they went, and arrived at a small pond. All the elephants drank, including Ely whose drinking skills were most impressive. Now nearly eight months old, he was able to suck the water up with his trunk, carry it to his mouth, lift his head and pour the water into his mouth, hardly spilling a drop. While the others went off to feed on the surrounding palms, Ely stayed at the water's edge continuing

*Elspeth, Ely and Ella's calf, Esau, drinking with various degrees
of proficiency: Elspeth at two and a half only loses a few
drops, Ely at 15 months dribbles a respectable few drops, and
Esau at five months spills more than he swallows.*

to drink. Eventually he appeared to get bored and started splashing the surface with his trunk and spilling water that he had sucked up.

In the meantime, Echo had managed to dig out a heart of palm with her tusks, which is a difficult task, and one she seems to specialise in. She was standing by herself, obviously relishing her feast, when M22 started to walk through the glade. He literally did a doubletake when he smelled Echo's palm heart. He stopped short, made a right-angled turn and headed straight for her. M22 is nearly a metre taller at the shoulder than Echo and probably weighs about twice as much and I assumed that if he wanted her palm heart, he would get it. I underestimated Echo. When she saw that M22 was coming, she picked up the heart and ran off with it. Ely saw his mother hurry away and, quickly trying to join her, ran directly into M22's path, which sent him into even more of a panic. A brief moment of chaos ensued, with elephants going in all directions. The end result was that M22 gave up his pursuit and ambled off in a dignified manner.

Apart from such competition over food, there is usually little interaction or interesting behaviour to observe among elephants in the late dry season. Families tend to move on their own and may even split into subgroups. There are rarely any females in oestrus, only one or two males are in musth and there are usually no births between late August and late December. Thus it came as a great surprise to witness, on the following afternoon, an event that revealed new insights into the nature of elephants. We had spent the morning of 22 October with the EBs, and at 16:30 we set out to join them again by a route that took us out on the plain to the east of our camp. There we saw a small group of four elephants, which was strange because they would normally be in the swamps or woodland at that time. Although they were half a kilometre away, I could tell from their postures that they were disturbed – their heads were held high and their ears were raised and tense. As I watched, three of the elephants moved off to the east towards Longinye swamp leaving the largest animal behind. I drove along the road towards them and saw that the large animal was the 'right one-tusked' female, Grace of the GBs. The three individuals that had walked off were her calves: Gwen (11 years), Gail (eight years) and Garissa (three years and eight months). Next to Grace was a small pale object. I was just focusing on it with my binoculars when Grace bent down and, with her tusk hooked under it and her trunk holding it from above, lifted it in the air and carried it towards the other elephants. Then I saw that it was a tiny calf. Grace moved rapidly about 20 metres (65 feet) with her head held high and her tusk stuck straight out, until the calf slipped out of her grasp and dropped more than 1.5 metres (5 feet) through the air, landing hard on the ground. The others must have heard something because they all turned round and came running back to Grace, and milled about with much rumbling and earflapping.

I spoke to a driver who said that the elephants had been there since morning when Grace had apparently given birth. The calf had been out in the hot sun all day, as well as falling at least once from a considerable height. I thought it must be dead, and left the road to drive over and check. The elephants were somewhat alarmed and defensive on our arrival, but soon ignored us. About a minute after we got there, we realised with a sickening feeling that the calf was still alive. Grace's oldest daughter, Gwen, tried to lift it and the calf, a female, twitched and let out a weak groan. The scene brought back disturbing memories of Ely's first day, but this time there could not possibly be a happy ending.

The calf lying on the ground looked about half the size of a normal newborn. I doubted whether the pitiful little creature had ever stood and suckled. It was a strange greyish-pink colour rather than the healthy dark grey of a new calf, and was bleeding slightly from the eyes, mouth and genitals. From its size and colouring, I concluded that it was born prematurely. I later looked up the oestrus records and, although that sighting was not conclusive, it suggested that Grace had been in oestrus in May 1989 and was due to have a calf in March 1991. Therefore this calf was probably about four months premature.

Grace and her older calves were all extremely distraught. They frequently rumbled contact calls and one or two of them would set off towards Longinye only to turn round and come back after going 10 or 20 metres (33–65 feet). I marvelled at the bonds between mother and calf, and between the older calves and their mother. The other members of

Grace carries her premature and dying calf
towards the seclusion of the woodlands.
In the end she carried it over half a kilometre
and hid it deep in a clump of palms.

the GB family were probably within vocal distance, and food and water were nearby, but the juveniles remained, thirsty and hungry, on the open plain. Those bonds must be very beneficial to have evolved to that extent.

A pair of jackals was circling at a distance of about 50 metres (160 feet). The older elephants kept raising their heads and taking threatening steps towards them. Gwen tried several more times to lift the calf by gently nudging it with her foot and wrapping her trunk around it. As soon as it made a sound, Grace pushed Gwen aside and bent down to it herself. Three times over the next hour she lifted it on to her tusk and carried it until it dropped to the ground with a horrible thud. Each time she headed towards the woodlands of Ol Tukai Orok near my camp. Although I had read reports of females staying with their dead babies and carrying them, I think in this case, Grace was stimulated to carry the calf and not leave it because it was alive and every once in a while moved or gave a weak cry. As we were leaving them, well after sunset, Grace picked up the calf again and managed to carry it another 30 metres (100 feet).

The next morning we went out before dawn to find that Grace and her calves were no longer on the plain. We searched around the area and spotted Gwen and Gail at the edge of the palm thickets of Ol Tukai Orok. When we had driven over to them, we could make out Grace and her three-year-old, Garissa, inside the palms. By further manoeuvring the car, we could just see the tiny calf on the ground beside them. Grace had carried the calf over 500 metres (1600 feet) to the seclusion and cool of the thick palms. It was an amazing feat of dexterity and determination.

We thought that the calf was dead, but could not see well enough to be sure. In the course of the morning, there were frequent rumbling calls. Grace barely moved from the calf, only going out of the palms briefly three times. She was followed each time by Garissa, who had been trying to suckle the previous day and had been refused. On this day, Grace allowed her to drink. At noon Grace disappeared and we took the opportunity to go up to an opening in the palms and look in. The calf was lying on its brisket, no longer breathing. The ground around it was very dug up indicating there had been a great deal of disturbance in the area. Fifteen minutes later Grace and the others came back, having been to the swamp to drink. They took up their vigil once more and stayed near the dead calf for the rest of the day.

We spent the following day with the EBs, but checked on Grace when we went in and out of the camp. On the second occasion she was away from the calf and we could see that it was partially eaten. It was probably the jackals that had got to it. Lions or hyenas would have finished the carcass unless interrupted by Grace. On 25 October, three days after the birth, Grace was still in the area. She was no longer standing over the calf, but was going back to it from time to time.

We sighted the GBs on 27 October and 2 November, both times without Grace and her calves. It was not until 7 November that I recorded the whole family together again. Thus Grace had spent at least three days guarding her dead calf and had been separated from her family for two weeks. I wondered how much of that time they were in vocal communication with each other. We know that many of the rumbles that the elephants make are of very low frequency, too low for human hearing. These infrasonic calls carry great distances, possibly as far as 10 kilometres (6 miles). It could be that Grace was in fairly regular contact with the rest of her family. Indeed, while Grace was with the dead calf we heard elephant calls from her direction. We can recognise and describe many of the sounds that elephants make, but we do not yet know what messages they are conveying. I could only wonder whether Grace relayed any of the stress and disturbance she was undergoing.

Towards the end of October, rain clouds had started building up every afternoon, marching in from the east. On the 30th and 31st there was rain all around the Amboseli basin, on the slopes of the mountain and on the higher ridges to the east, but none fell in the park. Then on the afternoon of 7 November we had a brief storm of tremendous wind accompanied by only a little rain. Still, with only 300 millimetres (12 inches) of rain falling on average during the year, every drop counts. We woke on 8 November to a fresh clear day with everything looking sparkling and bright, having been washed clean by the rain. It was a day that we had set aside for paperwork and we forced ourselves to stay in the camp. Had we not done so, we might have missed a second fascinating yet sad event.

Kadzo, the Ph.D. student, had left camp early and returned around 11:30 to report a sick elephant among the AAs, a big family with 22 members. She had first noticed the young female at about 9:00, when the AAs were on the northern edge of Ol Tukai Orok. Astrid, the 11-year-old daughter of Alison, was kneeling down, urinating a lot, and appeared to have a very bad stomachache. Kadzo went off to do her work and came back to the family around 11:00. By then they had moved across the pan to the edge of Enkongo Narok swamp, leaving Astrid far behind. Her mother, Alison, kept going back to her, apparently urging her to come along.

From what Kadzo told us, I thought that Astrid might have an intestinal blockage or some other digestive disorder. However, similar behaviour I had seen once before prompted me to go to my tent and get out the records of oestrus and mating. I discovered that Astrid had been seen in oestrus on 16 December 1988, just over 22 months before when she was one month short of 10 years old. Although this would be young to start breeding, it was possible that Astrid was about to give birth.

Martyn and I leapt into the Land Rover and headed for the swamp. There we found most of the A As feeding in the swamp and on the shore. The 28-year-old adult female Alison and her two-year-old male calf were standing next to Astrid who was lying down in the mud and water. I had known Alison since she was 10 years old and watched her grow up to have calves of her own. Astrid was her second-born and her first to survive to maturity. For the next hour, Astrid stayed there, occasionally raising her head or standing up and lying down again. From the little we could see, she might have been in labour or she might have been ill. Then at 13:50, Astrid came out of the swamp. Her vulva was hanging down, covered in mud, and a small lump protruded below her tail. That clinched it: she was in labour.

This was only the third birth that had been witnessed in the history of the project, and I watched Astrid's behaviour very carefully. After coming out of the swamp, she moved to a clump of *Salvadora persica* bushes and beat them with her tusks. She was

---

*In the early morning light, the elephants
create an aura of mystery and
timelessness as they feed amongst the classic
umbrella trees of the savannah.*

holding her tail off to one side and urinating frequently, appearing agitated. Then she knelt down on her hind legs, straining several times. A few minutes later, she moved north with her mother about 30 metres (100 feet), picking leaves from bushes and eating a bit. Soon she started ripping apart a bush again, and I wondered whether this might be a reaction to the pain. At 14:09, Astrid lay down, but Alison rushed over to her rumbling and she got back up again. After another few minutes she was straining again, nearly kneeling.

Over the next couple of hours, she repeated these activities in varying order many times. Alison stayed close by but stopped encouraging her to stand after a while. Both elephants rumbled at each other and may have also been in vocal contact with the rest of the family, who had moved away, still feeding. By 16:40 the bulge below Astrid's tail seemed more pronounced and slightly lower, but otherwise there was little change.

The following extract from the detailed notes I took covers the next half hour.

16:44 Kneels down in squatting position again, really straining now.

16:45 Still in squatting position, holding quite still. For a first time mother she does not seem as agitated as I would have expected.

16:46 Down on all four legs like a dog. Then rolls over partially on her side. Amelia [another adult female from the AAs] and three calves approach from the south. Exchange of rumbles between Amelia and Alison.

16:50 Astrid stands up. Tail high up in the air. More rumbles from Amelia. Think the foetus is quite far down, part of it at least half way. Alison comes over to Astrid, reaches trunk towards her. Alison's calf arrives as well.

17:05 She's been squatting quite a lot. Several long squats. There is now a bit of blood coming from the vagina and we can see the full length of the foetus in the birth canal.

17:06 Squatting again. Her anus is pushed way out and the birth canal is tremendously distended. Other elephants from the family approaching. Alison staying close to her.

17:09 She's kneeling down again on her back legs, straining. Part of it is still high up. The mass of the foetus still seems to be up below the anus.

17:11 She just squatted again and I thought I saw the foetus slip down quite fast.

17:12 Back up, no longer squatting. Main bulge still up by her tail.

17:13 Squatting again down on her right rear knee. Alison staying close by.

17:15 Stands up. There's very little blood, just a few drops. She's kicking backwards. Her whole backend is protruding out about a foot.

17:22 Calf born.

The actual birth happened very quickly. At first, Astrid was partially obscured by a bush, and we could just see one hind foot and then another sticking out of her vulva. By good fortune, she then came out into the open and stood next to where we were parked. She gave one last push and the foetus was propelled forward with great force. It shot forwards, hind end first, and landed on its back. While its hindquarters up to the middle of its body were bare, the head and shoulders were covered in the foetal sac. Attached to the sac around its forehead was the placenta. The umbilical cord was wrapped around its chest. In the only other birth I had seen before, the calf struggled from the moment it was born. This calf lay still.

It was a large male calf with dark healthy looking skin. As soon as it dropped, Astrid backed over it and moved away with her trunk and ears out, looking very alarmed. Her mother, Alison, immediately came over to inspect the calf. She reached her trunk out and shook her head with a loud slap of her ears against her neck – a typical gesture of elephant 'disapproval'. She moved closer and gently nudged the calf with her foot and tried to lift it. The calf continued to lie still and we realised then that it was dead.

Virtually all elephant births at Amboseli take place at night and I suspected that Astrid had started in labour the night before or as long as 24 hours before. Perhaps it was a long labour because it was a breech birth or because the calf was large and Astrid was relatively young. Whatever the reason, I thought the calf had died as a result of the long labour, probably smothered by the umbilical cord around its chest.

While her mother tried to lift the calf, Astrid stood about 12 metres (40 feet) away, looking dazed. About eight minutes after the birth, she went back over to the calf, smelled

Eleven-year-old Astrid of the AA family
finally reaches the last stage of her long labour
as the calf's feet begin to emerge.

---

it and rumbled. In the meantime, Alison moved off in a purposeful manner heading north. Over the next 15 minutes two more females from the AA family arrived and smelled the calf. They seemed to know right away that it was dead, becoming quiet and hesitant in the way that elephants do when they come upon elephant bones or carcasses. Then the adult female Audrey arrived with her own calf, which was no bigger than the dead calf. She greeted Astrid by reaching her trunk towards her mouth, and smelled the calf. Afterwards she turned her back on it and very gently reached backwards and touched it with one hind foot, a gesture I have seen made to other dead elephants before. Audrey turned back round to face the calf and, bending down, ripped open the foetal sac with one

*The calf shoots forward, hind feet first
and lands on its back with the fetal sac
and placenta covering its head.*

of her tusks. Usually a calf kicks in the sac and females will help the mother remove the membrane. This time there was no movement and Audrey gave up after one tear.

Astrid was standing quietly nearby, sometimes picking up sticks and throwing them in a form of displacement activity. Then she came closer to the dead calf but still appeared to be frightened of it. At 17:55 a second wave of animals from the large AA family began to arrive. Astrid became more alert and, after being greeted by her relatives, started secreting from her temporal glands. I found it interesting that the secretions flowed in such social situations and not, for example, in the stress of labour.

By 18:00 Astrid seemed less exhausted and more disturbed. She stood right next to the baby and kicked up grass in an agitated manner. She was slightly aggressive towards the younger females from the family who tried to approach. It looked as though her maternal instincts had emerged and she was trying to defend the calf. One of the juvenile females placed a stick on the dead calf. Others were kicking at the grass and earth but there was no loose dirt there to place on the carcass.

At 18:12 Wart Ear, the matriarch of the AAs, arrived, which caused tremendous excitement in all the elephants present, particularly Astrid. She flapped her ears, made very loud greeting rumbles and, with her head lifted high in the air and her mouth wide open, she bellowed her distress. I have seldom seen behaviour that showed so explicitly the relationship of the matriarch to family members. Wart Ear reached her trunk towards Astrid's mouth, but did not try to lift the calf. Two minutes later Astrid's mother returned, and there were more rumbles and trumpets. Alison went straight to the dead calf and smelled it, while Astrid greeted her with deep bubbly rumbles.

All these interactions and behaviours were fascinating but also frustrating because I did not know what was going on in the elephants' heads. I found Alison's behaviour particularly intriguing. Throughout the birth she stayed with her daughter, barely eating anything and remaining calm and always at hand. As soon as the calf was born she was there to assist, presumably to help get it on to its feet. She then walked off in a purposeful way and came back very soon after Wart Ear arrived. But what had she been 'thinking' during the birth? Had she afterwards gone to fetch Wart Ear and, if so, why? I would love to know more about the cognitive processes of these complex animals.

Shortly after Alison returned, the last of the adult females in the family, Amy, arrived. Again, she greeted Astrid, and smelled and felt the dead calf. Like all the others, she seemed to know immediately that it was dead. Well after dark we left Astrid surrounded by her whole family, and benefiting from their concern and companionship. I felt sad for her, but knew she potentially had a long reproductive life ahead of her and the possibility of many healthy calves. She showed no sign of haemorrhaging and I felt confident she would recover quickly.

The following morning we revisited the birth place and came upon a very poignant scene. Astrid was standing next to the dead calf completely on her own in the wide open landscape. The calf had not been moved, although some grass had been placed on it. I was surprised that Astrid had stayed to guard her calf when her family and, particularly, her mother had left. Even at 11 years old and never having seen her calf alive, her maternal instincts were stronger than her social instincts.

When Martyn checked on Astrid again later in the morning she had left, but when I went out in the afternoon she was back with the calf. In a circle about 30 metres (100 feet) away from her were 20 vultures waiting patiently. The next day Astrid was back with her family and there was no sign of the little calf, nor of the drama that had taken place two days before.

On 11 November, Martyn and I went out to spend our last day with the EBs before taking another break. We would not be resuming our observations until January and thus, unfortunately, would miss the birth of Ella's calf. By my estimation Ella was now 21 months pregnant and would have her calf towards the end of December. Having just witnessed two unsuccessful births we hoped this one would go well. The first of the EBs we came across were Ella and three calves along the edge of Enkongo Narok. She seemed to be splitting from Echo more often these days, and looked very tired and slow. She kept stopping, vocalising and listening, but all her sounds were 'contact calls' and not 'contact answers', which probably meant she was not in vocal communication with Echo. Later we found Echo a couple of kilometres away with the rest of the family, all busily feeding on palms.

That afternoon we had a good rain storm and more rain fell in the night. I was relieved; I had begun to worry that there would be a failure of the short rains. There had been no rain of any consequence until this time and the park was showing the effects of the extended dry season. All the grass outside the swamp areas was completely finished and even at the moist swamp edges it was eaten down to a stubble.

DROUGHT

November 1990 to March 1991

November and December

During the remainder of November and most of December I was in Nairobi and relied on Kadzo, Norah and Soila for news of Amboseli. More rain came in November and the park turned green, but early in December the rains ended. On adding up the figures I found that the total rainfall for the short rainy season was a disappointing 66.2 millimetres (2.6 inches). In good years as much as 200 millimetres (7.8 inches) of rain fell in Amboseli during October, November and December. In some years, such as 1990, the 'between the rains' months of January and February received extra rain, and I hoped this would happen in 1991.

On 17 December, Norah came across the EBs while carrying out censuses of the family groups and bulls. All the members were present, apart from Emo. They were in Olodo Are, probably having moved out of their dry season home range in response to the rainfall. A few minutes after sighting them, she realised that there was a tiny calf with Ella. On closer inspection she saw that it was a male calf and estimated that he was about

Amboseli is famous for its fine alkaline dust which becomes a familiar feature during the dry season and an all-pervasive presence during a drought.

five days old. Although he had been born a few weeks earlier than we had expected, he did not look particularly small. He was not as big as Ely had been at birth, but this was probably just as well. Ella's calf looked normal, active, and healthy.

I went to Amboseli with several friends for Christmas, and was pleased to see that the grass had grown up in the camp and all looked well. During my short stay I tried twice to find the EBs but had no luck. Norah reported that there were few elephants in the park, and those that were tended to gather in large groups in Olodo Are. She had last seen Echo and her family on 21 December in Longinye among a group of 55 elephants.

January to March

Martyn arrived in Kenya on 8 January and we returned to Amboseli on the 11th. As at the beginning of 1990, the sky was a clear blue and Kilimanjaro seemed closer and more magnificent with no clouds to shroud it. January is my favourite month in Amboseli. The park is green, the elephants tend to gather in large herds, there is usually a lot of oestrous behaviour and musth activity, and baby elephants almost appear to be dropping out of the sky. The only nagging worry I had this year was that the clear skies held little promise of the much-needed extra rain.

On the following day we toured Echo's favourite haunts and, as usual, could not find her. Each time we returned after being away, it seemed to take us a couple of days to get back in touch with her routine. It was not until the next evening that we located her and her family just emerging from the Ol Tukai Orok woodlands. Everyone except Emo was there and they all looked well, including Ella's new calf whom I named Esau.

Over the next few days we saw the EBs regularly, and Emo was absent every time. He seemed to have made a definite break. His move towards independence was confirmed on 18 January when the EBs were feeding just at the edge of the camp. Echo and the family had been in the area since early in the morning. At midday, Emo arrived with another family, the CBs. I thought he would go over and join his family, and I wondered how they would react to him. However, he did not even approach them. He left the CBs and wandered off to the south on his own, never having been closer than 100 metres (330 feet) to his family. He looked too small at 10 years old to be on his own and I was concerned about whether he would make it through the vulnerable teenage years. I would probably only have intermittent sightings of him as he grew and matured through his teens and 20s, until eventually he settled into a bull area and became a large breeding male with a regular routine.

A week later, on 25 January, we had an encounter that gave me some insights into the lives of medium-sized independent males. That evening we were driving back to camp when we saw two bulls out on the open pan to the east of Ol Tukai Orok. I do not know the bulls nearly as well as the females, partly because I see them less regularly. Also, the males grow and change more rapidly than the females, and their ears seem to get more tears and holes in the course of time. I usually have to refer to the photographs on file in order to identify a bull. I did not immediately recognise either of these bulls, but something familiar about one of them made me stop the Land Rover.

They were both handsome, leggy bulls in their mid-twenties. By this age, the males are 30 centimetres or so (about a foot) taller than the biggest adult females, and their tusks are already thicker and heavier than those of any female. Despite his size and much thicker tusks, one of the bulls looked remarkably like Emo. I checked the file and confirmed that he was Little Male, Emo's older brother, who had left the family in 1983. I had not seen him, or at least had not been aware of seeing him, since 1989. I found it interesting that the sibling resemblance was so striking. It was also noteworthy that his companion was Ezra, who had left his natal family, the EAs, around the same time as Little Male. These two males had frequently been together when they were still in their families and were continuing to associate several years after independence. The records showed that they were not together consistently but that there was a tendency for them to be in the same bull group. Possibly males form stronger bonds than I had thought.

By Little Male and Ezra's age, bulls are just beginning to try to compete for females.

They are what is known as 'sneaky copulators'. In their mid-twenties, males are not big enough or strong enough to fight outright for oestrous females, and thus they have to adopt other strategies to secure matings. One technique is to find an oestrous female and mate with her before the big males find her. Another is to hang around when she is being guarded by a large musth male in the hope that he will be distracted by, for example, a potentially dangerous rival. While the big male is busy chasing off another big male, the sneaky copulators rush in and attempt to mate with the female.

We were keeping an eye on the older males too during this season because we wanted to film a male in musth. We came across two musth bulls in January, M10 and M132 (Chris). However, our first choice for the role was the striking and highly tolerant M22. In 1990 we had admired his skill in tracking down oestrous females during his musth period and spent an enjoyable few days with him in June during his retirement phase. This year we wanted to follow his musth activities in more detail. We were reasonably hopeful because M22 had a fairly predictable sexual cycle. We had musth records for him going back to 1977, and these showed that he had been in musth from January until March or April for the past 13 years.

This January we found him still in his bull area which, conveniently, was the Ol Tukai Orok woodland and Enkongo Narok swamp, the same general range that the EBs used. He showed none of the obvious characteristics associated with musth. He was usually on his own or in the vicinity of other bulls or family groups, and did not appear to be interested in females. On looking carefully at him I thought he seemed thinner than bulls

---

The Amboseli elephants share their range and their resources with a host of other grazing species including zebras and wildebeests. During hard times there is serious competition for the remaining vegetation.

usually do at the onset of musth. I could not see any sign of illness but felt that he was not in prime condition, which made me less confident that he would come into musth over the next weeks.

So far this January there had been no rain at all and the park was already drying out. On 26 January there was rain all around the basin, but not in the park. Five days later we had a good storm with 25.8 millimetres (just over an inch) of rain. Unfortunately, that was the last rain we had for a while. Over the next few weeks the Amboseli animals began to concentrate around the central swamps, as they did in the late long dry season months of September and October. The elephants came in early each day and went straight into the deep swamps. Soon after, the swamp edges were packed with wildebeests, zebras, buffaloes, and Thomson's gazelles. Once again my camp became a favourite grazing area, and the grasses that had stood 60 centimetres (2 feet) high at Christmas time were eaten down to a few centimetres.

I thought I had never seen so many wildebeests and zebras in Amboseli and the ecologist, David Western, confirmed that this was so. He had been working in the park for over 20 years and his counts showed that these two species had more than doubled in numbers since 1977. That year marked a turning point for many of the animals in Amboseli. It was the end of a long drought which had been particularly severe in 1976. It was also the year that the Maasai left the park permanently to live on group ranches on the surrounding land. With them went their livestock herds, which had been competing with the wildlife for grazing. Good rainfall over the next seven years and the absence of the Maasai herds, allowed the grazing species to flourish, including the wildebeest, zebra and buffalo. Elephant numbers had also increased, the elephant population having risen from 479 at the beginning of 1978 to 755 at the beginning of 1991. Thus the park was by now supporting a very high density of wildlife. Ecologists would probably have said that it had reached 'carrying capacity', which is the maximum number of animals a particular area can support. I am wary of this concept because I think conditions in African savannahs are too variable to arrive at a single maximum number. However, I concede that at a given time and with a given rainfall, there is a limit to the capacity of an area. In 1991 Amboseli appeared to have reached that upper limit.

In February the wildebeests began to drop their calves. Wildebeests have a relatively short, highly synchronised birth season, most giving birth in a period lasting approximately three weeks. It is thought that all the calves are born at about the same time in order to swamp predators. With hundreds of other calves available to the predators, each female's calf has a better chance of surviving. Virtually all the adult females appeared to have conceived in 1990 and soon there were dozens of new calves in each herd that we drove by. Just at the entrance to my camp, there was an area that rose into a large grassy knoll covering about a hectare and this knoll seemed to be one of the wildebeests' favourite birthing places. Each morning as we came out of camp there were new calves lying wet on the ground or struggling to stand, and often one or two females actually in the process of giving birth. At first, we found the scene exciting, but soon, like the predators, we became blasé about the calves. We were also aware that there would be a couple of thousand new mouths trying to feed on grass already reduced to a stubble.

By the middle of February, M22 still showed no signs of coming into musth and very few female elephants were coming into oestrus. In all of January and the first half of February only two females were recorded in oestrus, both of which had lost calves. One of them was Grace, who was apparently making up for the loss of her premature calf. We saw her in consort with the big musth male, M10, on 12 February. We wondered if Astrid would also come into oestrous soon.

On 14 February we left for Nairobi and Martyn went on to the UK for two weeks. During my time away from Amboseli, I asked Norah and Soila to keep a close watch on M22 and send me a message as soon as he came into musth. They reported that, although other males remained in musth and new ones were still coming into musth, M22 stayed in his bull area, looking decidedly uninterested in anything except eating. They did not see any females in oestrus during those two weeks, and there was no rain.

The lack of sexual activity during January and February was unusual. For example, in 1990, 26 females were recorded in oestrus during these months. The short rains brought up grasses, herbs and creepers, which the elephants ate and benefited from, and many responded to their improved condition by starting their sexual cycle. However, when Martyn and I drove into the park on 1 March, I understood the reason for the cessation of reproductive activity. I had not seen the park looking that desiccated in March since the droughts of 1976 and 1984. In addition to the extreme dryness, it was *very* hot. When we arrived at the camp the thermometer in my tent, in the shade of a thatched roof, read 37°C (98°F). The highest temperature I had recorded in my tent previously was 33°C (91°F). Later I learned that in Nairobi, the temperature also reached the high 30s for several days, breaking a 55-year-old record.

Elephants appear to have a built-in birth control system which responds to environmental pressures. The drought conditions around us that March had been building up since 1990. The long, hard dry season in that year had been followed by low rainfall during the short rains and almost no rainfall during January and February. In addition, the elephants faced increased competition from the rapidly expanding populations of wildebeests, zebras and other grazers.

In response, the females, with a few exceptions, had stopped their cycles altogether. The few males who did come into musth stayed in for shorter periods than usual and, notably, M22 did not come into musth at all on his regular schedule. My colleague Joyce Poole, who had specifically studied musth, thought that M22 had probably not fully recovered from his taxing musth period in 1990.

Many people do not seem to appreciate the degree to which elephants are tuned to environmental conditions. It is frequently stated that elephants can no longer live in most parks and reserves in Africa without drastic measures being taken to control their numbers. Given a restricted area, it is claimed, elephants will continue to reproduce and increase in numbers until they 'eat themselves out of house and home'. The latter phrase appears with great regularity in the popular press and in TV documentaries, yet there is no sound evidence that this has *ever* happened in Africa.

*M 22 feeding in one of the small swamps
near the camp and uncharacteristically showing
no signs of coming into the active 'musth'
phase of his yearly cycle.*

In Amboseli, my data on the elephant population over a 20-year period have shown that, as numbers increase and resources become scarce, the elephants' reproductive patterns change. Given the best of all conditions, with more than enough food for every elephant, a population might be able to grow at a rate of 6–7 per cent. That theoretical maximum assumes that no elephant dies until it reaches old age, and that females start conceiving at nine or ten years old and give birth to a calf every three years. In reality, these sets of circumstances probably occur very rarely and, even if they did, would not go on forever. With the exception of the rainforests, environmental conditions in Africa are highly variable with good years, bad years and everything in between. Elephants respond rapidly to these varying conditions, as had been pointed out by scientists working on other elephant populations before I began my study. When elephants become nutritionally stressed, females reach sexual maturity at a later age and may even delay until they are 18 or 19 years old. Instead of having a calf every three or four years, adult females in high density populations might have a calf every six, seven or eight years. In addition, in drought years the calf mortality might be as high as 50 per cent. All these parameters have a profound effect on the growth rate of a population, reducing it to 2–3 per cent or even zero and below. The chances of elephants eating themselves out of house and home is actually very unlikely.

When Martyn and I realised how bad conditions had become in Amboseli, we were anxious to see how the EBs were faring. On the day after we got back, 2 March, we set out to explore the central swamps. We found Echo and her family in Longinye, feeding in the deep swamps along with most of the other central families. The flow of fresh water from Kilimanjaro assured that the swamps would never dry up and some vegetation would continue to grow. However, with so many animals concentrated in a small area the growth could not keep up with the demand from the many grazers.

Although elephants are large and need proportionally greater quantities of food, they have the advantage that they can utilise areas and vegetation that other species cannot reach. They can wade right into the deepest swamps and feed on the coarse swamp sedges. They can break off branches from acacia trees and eat the twigs, leaves, bark and even the branches themselves. They can tear off the strong fronds of the *Phoenix* palms and chew on these, getting out the nutritious juices, and then spit out the undigestible fibre in a neat ball. The biggest of the elephants can reach the palm dates and their succulent outer pod covers. This March, the elephants were utilising all these sources yet there was still not enough to go round.

Echo and the members of her family were not gaunt but were looking thin. Their hip bones stuck out more than usual and their bumpy spines were more pronounced. The calves appeared to be reasonably healthy, which was a relief because calves are the most vulnerable members of an elephant population during a drought. Ely and Ella's calf, Esau, were at a particularly critical age. Ely had reached his first birthday on 28 February, while Ella's calf was not yet three months old. My records on calf mortality have shown that in low rainfall years it is the calves up to about a year old that are most likely to die. When they are well into their second year they seem to have a better chance of survival. Newborn calves are probably vulnerable because they rely solely on their mother's milk. If the mother does not get enough food she may not produce a sufficient quantity of milk or her milk may not be rich enough. When they are over four months old, calves have to supplement their milk diet with vegetation, but can handle little other than grass or soft leaves. During a drought, there may be no food available that they can eat. Once a calf is over a year old it is better able to deal with coarse vegetation and therefore is less at risk.

How well Esau and Ely did during this drought would depend heavily on Echo. In a normal or good year, the matriarch in an elephant family plays an important role, but in a drought year, her knowledge and experience can be crucial to the very survival of family members. Over the next few days, Echo led her family to the Longinye swamp each morning where they cooled themselves with the mud and water, drank and fed. Ely ploughed right into the swamp with the rest of them, plucking up the thinnest sedges and searching for creepers and other soft vegetation. He was coping well for his age, but then he had always been very precocious in his feeding and drinking abilities. However, Esau was not yet old enough to feed on the vegetation and was clearly reluctant to spend the day in the swamp. Much of it was too deep for him and he had to swim around from one clump of vegetation to another to keep up with Ella.

On one morning, the EBs went to the edge of the swamp where there was a steep bank alongside a stretch of open water and an area of thick floating vegetation. Ella lowered herself off the bank and slowly made her way out through the lily pads and clumps of sedges to feed, while Esau stayed on the bank with the family. Gradually most of the rest of the group joined Ella apart from two allomothers. Esau suddenly appeared to notice that, except for his two companions, he had been deserted. By this time his mother was farther downstream, up to her ears in water and vegetation, and I was fairly sure that he could not see her. He ran along the bank calling with the deep, guttural, baby distress call. His allomothers followed, reached their trunks to his mouth and put their trunks over him, trying to draw him near, but he was inconsolable. He ran upstream, calling, followed by the allomothers, and soon the three of them were racing up and down the bank more and more frantically. Every so often Esau would stop and listen, then run on. Eventually he must have heard something (presumably an infrasonic call since it eluded us) because

Emma with her new brother, Esau. Enid had
monopolised Ely, rarely letting anyone
else look after him, but when Esau was
born Emma finally had 'her own' calf
to take care of.
Opposite: *At dawn, a large bull is already up*
and trying to find the tastiest morsels.

he moved farther downstream and hurriedly scrambled down the bank. He plunged in and after a hard struggle, half swimming and half clambering over vegetation, he reached his mother.

The EBs visited Longinye for the next two weeks, keeping more or less to the same routine. They probably did not feed very much in the night because there was virtually nothing to eat outside the swamps to the east where they appeared to be spending the night. We usually found them resting in a large patch of *consimilis* grass to the north of Longinye each morning. Generally they woke up by midmorning and made their way to the swamp just as it was starting to get hot. Their movements may have been influenced by the Maasai and their cattle, as well as the drought and heat. While a water pipeline was under repair the Maasai were being allowed to bring their cattle into the park to drink. The cattle were supposed to come in, drink and leave again immediately. The Maasai were fairly good about keeping to the agreement, in this part of the park at least, and did not allow the cattle to move farther along the swamp edges to graze.

The presence of the Maasai in and around the park is a mixed blessing. They have lived in Amboseli for the past 400 hundred years or more and, without them, there would probably be far less wildlife left. While agriculturists could not possibly share their maize fields with families of elephants, the pastoralist Maasai can co-exist with them. Their herds of cattle, sheep and goats compete with the wildlife for food, but otherwise they live in relative harmony. On the other hand, the Maasai spear and kill elephants every year. Since the men walk around in the bush with just their spears for protection, and the women often walk with no protection at all, it is understandable that they wish to keep dangerous animals at a distance. The system seems to work fairly well, for the elephants are terrified of them. Kadzo's study of the relations between the Maasai and the elephants showed that the cows and calves especially run whenever they hear or smell Maasai at close range. She found that the bulls, for some as yet unknown reason, were far less frightened of the Maasai.

While the EBs were in Longinye we often observed their nervousness of the Maasai.

The sounds of cattle bells would always make them raise their trunks, smelling in the direction that the sound came from. If they heard the bells when they were out of the swamp, they would get into a defensive formation, usually a circle or semicircle, with the adults facing out towards the danger and the smallest calves hidden under and behind the bigger animals. These moments helped us to appreciate the evolution of the elephants' social system and the all-important family bonds.

By mid-March conditions had become very harsh, and I felt great sympathy for the Maasai and their animals. The livestock were forced to follow a three-day drinking regime. The Maasai grazed their cattle on the pitiful amounts of grass remaining out on the ridges for two days with no water at all, then drove them the long way into the park to drink before taking them back out again for another two days. Their cattle looked like skeletons with old rugs thrown over them as they walked in to water across the dry pan from several kilometres away. Each day we would see the long plumes of dust from herd after herd slowly marching in. Out on the ancient lake bed the shimmering heat haze turned them into weird and wonderful shapes.

Many of the cattle were dying and so were other animals. Most of the 1991 crop of wildebeest calves had very short lives, presumably because their mothers did not have the milk to sustain them. Adult wildebeests were dying too, as were zebra adults and foals, and a few buffaloes. The park became full of decomposing bodies and began to smell revolting, including the area around the small swamps near my camp. The hyenas and vultures had a continual feast awaiting them, but the hyenas appeared to prefer fresh meat. They did a lot of hunting, although the wildebeests were so weak that it was probably more like knocking over a stuffed dummy. Unfortunately, the knoll at the entrance to the

Overleaf: *The drought progressed and by mid-March the park looked barren and desiccated.*

camp became one of their favourite restaurants. I started calling it 'the killing fields', but as the drought got worse and more and more animals were just keeling over there I renamed it 'death knoll'. Each morning when we drove out there was always something gruesome to behold. The worst were the baby wildebeests unable to stand but not yet dead, lying flat out surrounded by 10 or more vultures. Every so often one of the vultures would get up the nerve to run in and peck the unfortunate calf, which would twitch and struggle until the vulture backed off. Mercifully, when we returned at midday the calf would be dead and, often, little trace of it would remain.

On 14 March the EBs abandoned Longinye and returned to Ol Tukai Orok. I had noted that some of the elephants in Longinye had diarrhoea and wondered whether a change of diet had become a necessity for the EBs. Having concentrated on swamp vegetation for over two weeks, Echo and the other adult females now spent what seemed like the whole day with their heads deep in palms. These big animals had no trouble tearing off the huge palm fronds and chewing them. The older calves fed on the palms as well for short periods, but appeared to tire quickly and begin to search round for other vegetation hidden below the palms. The younger calves had the most difficulty. Ely, Edgar, Elspeth and Emma were not strong enough to break off the fronds. They sometimes picked up bits that their mothers dropped and chewed on these but it seemed that their teeth and jaws were unable to deal with the fronds' tough, spiky fibres. Whenever the family got close to any of the small swamps in Ol Tukai Orok, these young calves would head straight for them and feed on the soft vegetation.

The small calves were also at a disadvantage when the adults and older calves started feeding on the underground roots of several species of grasses that grew in the area. It took a great deal of patience and dexterity to dig these roots up. A combination of pulling and twisting with the trunk while digging and kicking with the toes of one foot was necessary to dislodge the root. Once a clump of short grass and roots was freed, the elephant had to clean off the dust and earth by rubbing it against a leg or mashing it with the trunk and tusk, and shaking it. Finally, when it was in a suitable condition for eating, it was placed in the mouth. The whole process could take over a minute. It was a lot of work for a very small reward, but these were desperate times. Of course, the youngest calves did not yet have this skill. One day we watched with respect as Elspeth worked at small clumps of grass, trying to learn this feeding technique, and succeeding. Ely, on the other hand, stood right under Elspeth's chin and picked up anything she dropped, and sometimes reached into her mouth and pulled out a hard-won morsel.

The elephants occasionally resorted to more unusual food. In the late afternoon on 17 March we were with the EBs as they came away from the area in the woodlands I call Mamba Glade, because I once nearly ran over a 2.4 metre (8 foot) long black mamba snake there. The family was moving slowly and lethargically out towards the open pan, appearing to have no energy and no enthusiasm for any of their activities. Just watching them made us feel tired. Suddenly Ella's little calf, Esau, broke off from his mother, turned at right angles and headed south in a very purposeful manner. When he was over 20 metres (65 feet) from Ella he met Enid, whom he greeted briefly by reaching his trunk to her mouth, but immediately went on. Soon I saw that he was making a beeline for a fresh, steaming pile of dung deposited by Eudora a few minutes before. He knelt down, put his mouth right into it and started eating. Emma, Enid and Ewan had followed him, and Emma also started eating the dung, although in a more delicate fashion using her trunk. Enid and Ewan smelled the pile but did not partake.

I had seen both youngsters and adults eat other elephants' dung before. Very young calves eat their mother's dung in the first weeks, presumably to establish the intestinal micro-organisms necessary for digestion. It is not common for older animals to eat droppings, but every once in a while an adult is tempted. I think this behaviour occurs when another elephant has found something to eat that is rare and highly palatable. Since elephants only partially digest their food, some of the special treat emerges in the dung and is still appetising. During a drought, when small calves have such a difficult time handling the available food, eating pre-processed vegetation may be a good way to supplement a meagre diet. Whatever the reason, Esau and Emma seemed to be enjoying their meal.

After several days of eating palms and grass roots in Ol Tukai Orok, the EBs found a place that seemed to have been overlooked by the other animals. It was a grass-covered island about 2 hectares (5 acres) in size in Enkongo Narok swamp. Although dry and yellow, the grass was still relatively high. The island had been created by a channel of the swamp that was deep and fast flowing, more like a river than a section of swamp. The banks down to the river were steep, which had probably stopped wildebeests and zebras from crossing over to the island and eating down the grass. Perhaps other elephants were not using it because it lay just opposite the park boundary on the western side of the swamp, where the Maasai brought their cattle to drink and graze. Echo appeared to be willing to tolerate the potential danger and took her family there for several days in a row. Each night they came off the island and moved out to their night feeding and resting

Lowering himself into the swamp, a calf gets ready to feed on the coarse and not particularly palatable or nutritious swamp vegetation, but in a drought there is little choice.

Young calves sometimes split off from
their families to feed on the softer
more easily digested vegetation growing in
small pools in the woodlands.

areas to the south, and then returned very early in the morning to exploit one of the few areas of grass remaining.

We could not cross to the island and parked on the eastern bank of the river. From there we observed, on one day, the clearest demonstration of Echo's leadership we had ever seen. The family was spread out feeding, facing in all directions. Echo and some of her calves were drifting towards the river when she stopped feeding, gave a brief flap of her ears and made a low, throaty sound which I recognised as the 'let's go' rumble. The call did not immediately galvanise the other members into action – I do not think they had the energy for that – but they started moving towards her and the river, some still feeding as they walked and others striding more purposefully. Once everyone was approaching her, Echo headed towards the river bank. By the time she reached it others had moved ahead of her and had lowered themselves down the bank. To achieve this manoeuvre, each elephant had to step off the top of the bank, first with one forefoot then the other, shuffle a metre or so down and then kneel on the hind legs before one at a time placing each of these legs on the slope. Although well coordinated, elephants have to be very careful because a fall for an animal that heavy would have terrible consequences.

Once they were all safely down the bank, they crossed the river at a leisurely pace feeding on bits and pieces of plants and, possibly, simply enjoying the cold, rushing water. To get up the opposite bank, the reverse actions took place with each elephant kneeling on its front legs. At the top they stopped to dust themselves and then Echo led them off. She headed north across a plain but was soon stopped by Ely who wanted to suckle. In typical elephant mother fashion, she stood patiently while he latched on to a nipple and sucked noisily. The others went ahead about 20 metres (65 feet), and then also stopped. However, they were not just standing or resting on the plain, they were waiting.

Like so much of elephant behaviour this distinction was revealed in very subtle clues. Each of the adult females stood with her head turned back at a slight angle, presumably watching Echo. They swished their trunks to and fro, and Ella swung her foot back and forth, which is a classic sign of indecision among elephants. After about five minutes, Echo joined them with some low rumbles of greeting. Once again she gave the 'let's go' rumble, pushed through the group and led her family to the north-west. She took them across the hot, open plain and eventually arrived at an arm of Enkongo Narok swamp that we had not been to with the family before. There was some hesitation and what looked like a slight disagreement between her and Ella about where to go, with Ella starting off in one direction and, after a bit of rumbling back and forth, turning back towards Echo. Then they all waded into the swamp and started feeding.

As so often, I wanted to know what the elephants were 'thinking' during this time. There were many aspects of their actions I found puzzling. What prompted Echo to make the move? Why leave the island in the middle of the day? What did Ella want to do? What was influencing her behaviour? If the family made it through the drought, it would be due to Echo's leadership but how did her memories and experiences work on her decisions and behaviour? I could only speculate and remain intrigued.

From about the third week of March, clouds began building up every afternoon. These were the 'marching clouds' that heralded rain, coming in from the east in rows and squadrons. However they were not yet low enough or dark enough to produce moisture. With hungry animals and carcasses everywhere, Martyn and I became obsessed by the clouds and the hope for rain. On the afternoon of the 24th, the whole sky turned black to the east but the sun continued to shine in the Amboseli basin. This juxtaposition created some of the most beautiful scenes I have ever witnessed, with animals almost appearing to glow in the sunlight as they stood against the slate-grey backdrop. The rain was tantalisingly close but hot updrafts from the open pans pushed it away.

The next morning it was very hot and still, and by midday both Martyn and I felt heavy and slow. In the afternoon the sky blackened again, and this time the wall of clouds advanced despite the air currents, and its drenching, life-giving moisture poured down on Amboseli. We received 43.5 millimetres (1.7 inches) of rain in less than one hour. As soon as the first raindrop fell, sending up a puff of dust, the atmosphere changed. Our heads cleared and the weeks-long tension that the extremely dry air had created was dissipated.

The following day, 26 March, I flew to Nairobi. As the plane banked and headed north, I could see line after line of wildebeests and zebras heading out of the park to seek forage in areas without permanent water which they had been unable to use during the drought. Pools of water were dotted all over the landscape, glinting in the sunlight like dozens of huge mirrors. In an amazingly short time, the brown earth below me would turn a velvet green and the African savannah would once more become bountiful.

THE LONG RAINS

Late March to June 1991

Late March and April

After the storm on 25 March I kept my fingers crossed that it was indeed the beginning of the long rains. A few days later I was delighted to hear that on the afternoon of 29 March there had been a massive, nearly record-breaking storm in Amboseli. In less than three hours the park had received 88.5 millimetres (3.5 inches) of rain. Of course, this amount of water created problems, but one never complains about flooding in an arid area for fear of offending the 'rain gods'. It was wonderful to know that the rains were continuing.

The suspension of elephant reproductive behaviour during the drought meant that Martyn and I had still not adequately filmed oestrous, mating and musth, and all the activities that surround those events. It would take a while for the vegetation to grow up in response to the rainfall and much longer for the elephants to get back into reproductive condition. It seemed that when the females', and probably also the males', body fat reserves

Amboseli is perhaps the best place in Africa to observe elephants in all their majesty, the kings and queens of the savannah.

went below a certain level, their sexual cycles stopped. As their diets improved, they would start putting on weight and building up their fat reserves. Therefore, Martyn and I decided to resume our intense day-by-day observations at the end of May, when the park and animals should have recovered.

I returned to Amboseli on 4 April for a brief stay and, as I flew in, could not believe my eyes. There was more standing water in the park than I had seen since the heavy rains of 1978. Lake Amboseli was truly a lake with water stretching over 5 kilometres (3 miles) from north to south and 7–8 kilometres (about 4.5 miles) from east to west. A normally dry pan in the centre of the park was now also a huge lake. Once on the ground, I found new rivers flowing in unexpected places and many roads completely under water. I could barely get into the camp and was seriously worried about our ability to stay there if the water came up any higher.

I managed to get out into the park that afternoon but was restricted in where I could go and there seemed to be few elephant groups around. Thus I was pleased to see, on the afternoon of 5 April, a group of 15 elephants come into the glade to the south of the camp. I was even more delighted when, on closer inspection with my binoculars, I discovered it was Echo and her family, although Emo was still not with them. They were reddish in colour, and seemed alert and somewhat agitated or stimulated. They were flapping their ears and most of them were secreting from the temporal glands. I suspected the migratory urge was upon them. Their colour indicated that they had been up on the red soil ridges to the south or east of the park. After feeding briefly, they moved on to the south-east.

I returned to Nairobi soon after and went off to the USA and Canada for a month to give some lectures and visit family and friends. I felt a bit guilty about leaving Kadzo, Norah and Soila to deal with the potentially flooded camp. Fortunately, although more rain came, there was not another heavy storm, and they and the camp remained more or less dry.

May and June

On 22 May, eight weeks after the first rains fell, Martyn and I drove from Nairobi to Amboseli. We crossed the Athi-Kapiti plains, which were as green as an Irish meadow, down through the rolling hills of Kajiado district, where the Maasai cattle looked fat and shiny, to the town of Namanga nestled under hulking Ol Donyo Orok, the black mountain. Then we entered Amboseli, passing the Ilaingurunyeni hills before reaching the edge of the lake. It was still full of water glittering in the sunlight and offering an upside-down view of Kilimanjaro. In the park, every bush was in full leaf and the grass was over 30 centimetres (1 foot) high. There was not a wildebeest or zebra in sight; these and other grazers were still feeding on the more nutritious grasses outside the basin.

After fording a tricky section of road which had turned into a river, we reached the camp and discovered that a new entrance had been cut through the palms because our old drive was under water. The camp itself was just high enough to escape the surrounding 'lakes' and was looking very beautiful. Peter, the camp manager, and his assistant, Wambua, had kept everything in good condition – the grass was so well manicured it looked like a golf course. It was good to be back.

Soon after our arrival, Norah and Soila came over to tell us the elephant news and gossip. A number of females had come into oestrus, several males were in musth and 17 females had given birth. M22 had not come into musth, which did not surprise me. Being in musth outside his slot of January to early April would have put him in competition with other high-ranking bulls. Instead he appeared to have simply skipped one year. Among the bulls in musth were the biggest, M13 (Iain), the fourth largest, Patrick (M45), plus M5, Masaku and Ed. It sounded as though there would be reproductive behaviour in abundance.

Just before sunset we went out for a short drive and, contrary to our usual experience, we came upon the EBs immediately. Echo and the family were close to the camp on the eastern edge of Ol Tukai Orok, some out on the plain and others back in the palms. From

Above and below:
When the rains finally came, the elephants
took on a new lease of life and at every
opportunity exhibited their good condition:
two calves play a game with a stick; and
in the absence of a suitable playmate
Esau devises his own game.

*A female and her two calves feed at the edge
of Longinye swamp. The rain had brought up
fresh new grass, ensuring that there was enough
food for adults and calves alike.*

the woodlands we could hear sounds of calves playing, trumpeting and bashing through palms. We drove up and stopped next to where Echo was standing. She had an old palm frond in her trunk and was swishing it back and forth. Much to my delight I realised she too was being playful. She took one look at the car and, with a glint in her eye, came over with her head down in a mock charge, trumpeting the deep, nasal play trumpet. It was wonderful to see big stately Echo being 'silly'. She gave one more charge, then turned and walked off in a jaunty play gait. Nothing could have shown more vividly that she was relaxed and in prime condition.

The concept of adult play in animals is intriguing. Behavioural scientists have argued and discussed the topic without coming to a definite conclusion. Generally, play is restricted to juveniles of a species and it is thought to be mainly a means of learning skills needed in adulthood. For example, kittens go through developmental stages in which they play-fight with their siblings, chase each other, stalk and ambush one another, and eventually pounce on make-believe prey. Baby elephants also appear to be practising for adulthood when youngsters spar face to face, or one chases and mounts another. However this theory does not explain play among mature animals which have already acquired skills needed for adult life. One suggestion is that such play helps to maintain bonds among individuals living in social groups. It does appear that adult play is more common in social species, such as lions and porpoises. Another suggestion is that play is a means to expend excess energy. Certainly elephants only play when they 'feel good', that is, when they are nutritionally fit. Perhaps it is a combination of the two, plus an active, complex intelligence.

The following morning we got an early start, feeling exhilarated about the condition of the park and the elephants. We soon came upon a large, loose aggregation of about 150 elephants coming in from the south through the strip of *Acacia tortilis* trees and spreading out on to the open grassland to the south of the Serena Road. About a dozen families were there, including the EBs, and many bulls of all ages. Like the park, the elephants were transformed, in this case from the bony, slow, lethargic animals of the drought months to rounded-out, almost sprightly, creatures walking with vigour and verve. As always with an aggregation of this size, there was a lot of activity. Females were greeting other females, young males were sparring, calves were playing, and males were blatantly testing or surreptitiously smelling females, depending on the male's size and status.

It was soon obvious that there were one or two 'interesting' females present because most bulls had gravitated towards their vicinity. One of them was Eudora who was being a bit coy, moving off quickly when the males tried to approach her. When she stopped and urinated, the biggest male present, M5, went over to the large pool of liquid left on the ground. He tested it by smelling it and then placing the tip of his trunk in his mouth where there is an organ that assesses the hormone content of the female's urine. Eudora did not seem to be truly appealing since he did not pursue her. The other female who was showing some signs of being in oestrous was Odette of the OA family. She was being pursued by some of the young males, but not with much determination.

Having found Eudora uninteresting, M5 moved on to Odette. He was approaching her when he suddenly turned and lifted his trunk to smell in the direction of the acacia trees. We too looked in that direction and saw that the dynamics were about to change. Through the strip of trees, a massive bull was arriving. Even from 100 metres (330 feet) away I could tell that he was in musth. He carried his head high with his chin tucked in and his ears partially spread. As he strode out on to the plain, the overall impression he gave was one of tremendous size, power, and self-assurance. When he got closer the more conspicuous signs of musth became apparent: the bull's temporal glands above and behind his eyes were very swollen and down the sides of his face flowed a thick viscous fluid; he dribbled a continuous stream of urine, which left a trail as he walked, wet the insides of his legs, and turned the sheath of his penis a greenish white colour. When he arrived upwind of us his smell almost knocked us sideways. It was a pungent, sharp, somewhat musky scent which I had grown rather partial to.

This bull was Patrick in full and glorious musth. Even after years of watching bulls change from non-musth to musth, I am still impressed and intimidated by the Jekyll and

Hyde transformation. We had last seen Patrick on 22 March feeding peacefully in his bull area with a companion. At that time he was calm, conservative in his movements, and was concentrating on feeding, showing no interest in anything else that was going on around him. Now he was a swaggering, macho bully. The younger bulls discreetly moved out of his way and started casually feeding, turning away from the females as if they had no interest in them whatsoever. Patrick only had to turn towards M5, his sole potential rival, and emit a strange, deep, gurgling rumble while waving his ears, to make M5 move rapidly away.

Having taken care of M5, Patrick turned his attention to us. He came straight over to the vehicle, stopped, stood towering over us, and then suddenly dropped his head and charged. I hit the side of my door with my hand to create a loud bang and he skidded to a stop. I started the engine and withdrew with somewhat jellied knees and my adrenaline flowing. I explained to an ashen-faced Martyn that bulls in musth were unpredictable. Some of them tended to be very tolerant, like M22, while others seemed to consider the Land Rover another rival, or at least an irritant. My colleague, Joyce, discovered that bulls in musth have testosterone levels four times higher than those not in musth. The hormone testosterone is linked with aggressive behaviour in many mammals, including humans.

After seeing us off, Patrick went to work on the females. He started with the family nearest to us, the EBs. Being an experienced male, he did not just force his way into the family and start testing. He approached the females with what I have called 'the casual walk' holding his head lowered slightly and his trunk draped over one tusk. I think the posture conveys that no aggression is intended. His approach caused some excitement in

Patrick in full and glorious musth charges the Land Rover. Bulls in musth are surging with the hormone testosterone and can be aggressive and unpredictable.

the family. As soon as they smelled him, Echo, Ella and Erin lifted their heads and rumbled 'the female chorus', a special vocalisation made by females greeting musth males. They reached their trunks towards his temporal glands and penis, flapped their ears and rumbled. A few of them urinated, including nine-year-old Enid who seemed to be particularly stimulated. After spinning around and urinating, she stood with her mouth wide open, bellowing. In the meantime Eudora was looking wary, watching him over her shoulder. Patrick went to Enid, Erin and Ella in turn and thoroughly tested their urine. Echo and Eudora had not urinated. He moved to Echo and reached to her vulva, gently touched and sniffed it, and walked on over to Eudora. She started to move away but then stopped. He rubbed his head on her backside and pushed against her until she urinated a small amount. He spent longer testing her urine than he had that of any of the other females. He sniffed it, placed the tip of his trunk in his mouth, closed his eyes somewhat like a wine connoisseur, reached his trunk down again and repeated the tasting another two times. In the end he walked away, apparently having decided that she was not 'ripe' yet.

Patrick went from group to group until he had tested every female between the ages of about nine to 60. None was judged to be interesting and he moved on, heading towards Longinye. We followed him, keeping a discreet distance, as he strode along with his head high, dribbling and secreting. Suddenly he stopped and began smelling the ground. We could not see anything on the bare patch of soil he was investigating, but he became visibly more tense and alert. He also began dribbling urine at a much faster rate, issuing a steady stream of liquid, instead of drops like those from a leaky tap. He set off at a much faster pace, covering ground at considerable speed with long purposeful strides. He crossed the main park road, ignoring all vehicles, and kept going in a fixed direction. He appeared to be following a scent trail. Every 100 metres (330 feet) or so he stopped and smelled the ground and, as he walked, he held his trunk close to the ground in front of him, moving it from side to side. When he got closer to the edge of Longinye where the grass was high he had more trouble keeping to the trail, but each time he faltered he searched round, found it again and went on.

We drove ahead of Patrick to get an idea of where he was going and discovered a lone male feeding in the swamp. It was Lexi, a one-tusked bull about eight years younger than Patrick. Normally there would be no contest between these two bulls, but Lexi was also in musth, as we could see from the temporal gland secretions on the sides of his face, and I did not know how he would respond to the older bull. Patrick was approaching from the south, while the wind was from the east, and Lexi was facing north. He was obviously unaware that Patrick was heading straight for him. As Patrick got closer and closer I began to fear for Lexi. He was in about a metre or so of mud and water, and would thus find it difficult to get away if he wanted to. When Patrick zeroed in on the unsuspecting bull, I held my breath. Lexi whirled round and, for one moment faced Patrick, spreading and folding his ears in threat. Then he thought better of it, and began to plough his way out of the swamp as quickly as he could. He manoeuvred cleverly to skirt the swamp and get round Patrick and, once into the open, he took off at a run. Patrick started after him but soon stopped, having made his point. Lexi was still running flat out when he disappeared over the horizon a kilometre away.

It is not necessary for a bull to be in musth in order to produce sperm, mate with females and father calves, but the state of musth appears to confer tremendous dominance advantages on an individual. Its role has sparked controversy among elephant biologists from time to time, but it is generally agreed that musth functions mainly as a form of advertising. Only bulls in good condition can come into musth and when they do they are communicating to both females and other bulls that they are healthy and strong, and that they are surging with aggressive hormones that will make them fight, if necessary to

---

Overleaf: *During and after the rains, elephants form large aggregations in which important social events take place, including the finding of mates.*

the death, with other bulls to attain matings with females. Bulls in musth are always dominant to non-musth bulls even if those bulls are bigger and older. Thus dominance ranks change according to the musth status of the males. When there are several males in musth at the same time, the younger ones will usually give way to the older ones. M5 was in musth when we found him with Eudora, but, as soon as he saw Patrick, he stopped dribbling urine and secreting from the temporal glands. Not wanting to challenge a more dominant male in musth, he switched off his signals while in the other bull's presence.

While a male in musth is broadcasting his condition, a female in oestrus is sending out a message to the males that she is available. Such communication is vital because adult male and female elephants live such disparate lives. Spending time in different areas, and in different social groupings, they could have a problem finding each other for mating. Amboseli is a small park and the elephants tend to concentrate near the swamps, but in habitats where elephants live at lower densities and are more spread out, the problem of finding mates could be serious.

A female is usually in oestrous for about four to six days. During that period there is a peak time when she is most likely to conceive just after ovulation, which I think occurs on the third or fourth day of oestrous. A female's aim during oestrous is to find and mate with the 'best' male available – that is, the male who will pass on the most beneficial traits to her offspring, making him or her a successful reproducer in turn. These traits might be anything from a healthy and robust constitution to large body and tusk size.

Males, on the other hand, are looking not for quality but quantity. Their goal is to mate with as many females as possible and thereby father as many calves as they can. Musth is the somewhat unusual strategy elephant males have arrived at for achieving this goal. Since female elephants can be in oestrous at any time in the year, it might seem sensible for bulls to search for and pursue females throughout the year. However, their very large body size probably makes the males unable both to obtain the correspondingly large amounts of food they need and to compete for females all year round. Instead each male spends three or four months of the year searching for oestrous females, mating with any he can find, guarding them, and fighting with other bulls to maintain his dominance rank or attain a higher one. It is exhausting work, allowing him little time to feed or rest. As time goes by, the bull loses condition and eventually goes out of musth. Our studies in Amboseli have shown that the older the bull is and the higher his dominance rank, the longer he can stay in musth. Also the higher ranking bulls are in musth during those months when there are the most females in oestrous.

Patrick has a very good slot, coming into musth in April, May and June, which are peak oestrous months. Only two higher ranking bulls come into musth at about that time: M13, who is usually in musth in March, April and May, and Bad Bull, who is active in June, July and August. Patrick's aims during musth are to find and mate with oestrous females and to avoid these two males. To keep away from the bigger bulls, he relies partly on their signals. A musth bull sends forth cues by means of both odour and sounds. He dribbles urine, leaving a scent trail, rubs the secretions of his temporal glands on trees and bushes, and emits low frequency but loud musth rumbles which can travel over long distances. There is good evidence to suggest that an elephant receiving these messages knows which individual has left the trail or made the rumble. How the receiver reacts depends on its sex, age and reproductive state.

Among the males, a considerably more dominant musth bull, a male in retirement, or a young bull not competing for females might ignore the signal. A medium-sized bull, one of the sneaky copulators, might follow the trail or move towards the sound to see if he can get in on the action. A lower-ranking musth male is likely to flee in the opposite direction. A male close in dominance rank might move towards the vocal signal or follow the trail in order to confront the other male, as Patrick did with Lexi. Generally, though,

An oestrous female, followed by her confused two-year-old calf and a very intent adult male, tries to outrun her pursuer. She is rejecting his advances in the hopes of attracting a larger male in his prime.

the signals help to keep the musth males from meeting one another and having potentially life-threatening fights.

Females picking up the signals have a different attitude. They frequently show excitement when they find the scent trails left by a musth male, stopping to smell the ground, sometimes rumbling and urinating in response. When they hear a musth rumble they may answer with a female chorus, parts of which are infrasonic. Since infrasound carries over some distance, the chorus may help the male to locate the females. Our studies in Amboseli suggest that the matriarch of a family containing a female in oestrus, particularly a young female, might follow the trail or move towards the sound of the musth rumble, thereby leading her young relative to a suitable mate.

On 25 May we were fortunate enough to witness some of the behaviour that is the culmination of all the signalling, searching and competition. We had a slightly late start, setting out at 7:00, and as we headed towards the main road we spotted a group of elephants just off the road to the south. It was the OAs and CBs, two families that form a close bond group, and with them were 11 adult males. Something was obviously going on. We drove closer and I saw that the two families and their retinue were moving slowly east towards Longinye. Most of the cows and calves were feeding on grass or *suaeda* bushes as they made their way. Some of the bulls were also eating, but most did not appear to be interested in food. Among the bulls was Patrick, still in full musth; M5 and Ed, both recently in musth but prudently not showing any overt signs; and eight younger bulls ranging in age from 17 to about 25. Among these younger bulls was Tolstoy, who sometimes joined the EBs.

The families stopped in a patch of long grass and began to feed more seriously. Soon a single female and her two-year-old calf were isolated and more or less surrounded by the 11 bulls. Not surprisingly, Patrick was the one closest to her. The female was Odette whom we had seen acting warily around bulls three days before. There was nothing conspicuous happening in the group. If one drove past this tableau, it would appear that there were simply 13 elephants spread out eating grass. Actually there were 13 tense and alert animals, all interacting and communicating with subtle postures, gestures and vocalisations. Although they were not necessarily facing her, all the bulls were intent on Odette. She was in oestrus and the males wanted to mate with her.

The behaviour of males around a potential mate is always amusing to watch. Their every move is very, very careful and with good reason. If an animal as big as an elephant makes a faux pas amid 5–6-tonne rivals, it could end in much more than tears. On this day the elephants we were watching performed what looked like a very slow dance, with a sidestep here and a few steps backwards there, each separated from Odette by the exact distance that was tolerable to the most dominant bull. There was frequent surreptitious sniffing, with a bull turning his trunk tip ever so politely towards Odette while appearing to be looking in the opposite direction.

In the usual course of events a female comes into oestrus as a result of changing hormone activity. In the first day or two, she attracts males and makes herself conspicuous by running away from males in a typical way I have called the oestrous walk. This walk often develops into a chase, sometimes by several males at the same time. Females are faster than males and can usually outrun their pursuers, but they may get caught and mated. On about the third day, a large male usually finds the female, mates with her and goes into consort with her. In Amboseli over 90 per cent of these consort or guarding males are in musth.

Odette appeared to be following the typical pattern and was now in a consort relationship with Patrick. He kept the other bulls from chasing and harassing Odette by guarding her and threatening the other males, while Odette kept in close proximity to Patrick and did not let herself get cut off by another male. The other 10 bulls had no hope of mating with Odette if Patrick stayed with her. However, if any distraction occurred, they were ready to rush in in a matter of seconds. They were waiting for any relaxation in his guarding or any ill-judged moves on her part.

We followed Odette and her family and suitors as they went on to Longinye where they drank and began feeding. I was fairly sure Patrick had mated at least once with her,

The young female Ute is tested by Sleepy, one of Amboseli's biggest males and here in full musth. He clearly finds her of considerable interest as he assesses the hormones in her urine with a special gland in his mouth.

*Another musth male, Thor, mates with
Penelope, the matriarch of the PA family;
her family rushes over to participate
in the mating pandemonium.*

but I thought he would probably do so again. We waited for several hours until, at 13:25, Odette initiated the mating sequence herself. She moved off looking back over her shoulder in the classic oestrous walk. All the other bulls had started to converge on her before Patrick woke up and realised what was happening. He quickly set off after her, simultaneously releasing his penis from the sheath. Since Odette seemed to know just what she was doing, he did not have to chase her very far. When he caught up, he laid his trunk along her back and she stopped walking. Then, with his chin on her backside, he levered himself up on his hind legs and rested his front feet just behind her shoulders. His 1.2 metre (4 foot) long penis, with muscles allowing directional control, had curved into an S-shape. He hooked the tip of the penis into her vagina and with a thrust upwards his long organ was deep inside her. She cooperated by standing still and there was no apparent movement during the 45 seconds until he dismounted. Then the real excitement started. Odette lifted her head, opened her mouth and started making very deep, pulsating, rumbling calls. At the same time most of her family arrived, screaming, trumpeting, rumbling, roaring and bellowing in a display called 'the mating pandemonium'. Her family reached their trunks towards her mouth, her vulva and the fluids on the ground, while Odette turned and touched Patrick's penis three times with her trunk.

Odette's post-copulatory rumbles and the mating pandemonium of her family could be heard over a wide area. Joyce and I have speculated that these calls broadcast the news that there is a female in oestrus to draw in more males and increase the chances that the biggest, most dominant male around will find and mate with her. While females of other species generally advertise their availability, it is unusual for whole families to participate in the mate-attracting effort as they appear to do in elephant society. Odette was already with one of the 'best' bulls in the population and thus she and her family had been fairly successful. There was a possibility, though, that their calls might attract an even 'better' bull in musth at that time, such as M13. However, by the following day Odette was out of oestrus, and we could expect a new calf in the OAs about 656 days later, sometime in April 1993.

Having successfully filmed oestrous and mating behaviour our goal was once again to find the EBs each day and spend time with the family. The EBs cooperated by being easy to find, but we often had difficulty getting to them. In contrast with our experiences during the months of drought, Martyn and I were being continually diverted by exciting elephant behaviour everywhere we went. There seemed to be females in oestrus around every corner and almost each day brought a new bull into musth. We found newborn calves in many of the groups we encountered and the families were gathering in spectacular aggregations. Fortunately, the EBs were joining aggregations and we could often both be with them and have the chance of seeing other elephants' behaviour as well.

It was a week after Odette's mating that we were seriously distracted from the EBs once again. We had made our usual start at sunrise and at 6:40, we found a large, loose herd of cows, calves and bulls coming down through the *Acacia tortilis* strip and out on to the grassland. There were about 200 animals in the aggregation including, on the far side, the EBs. We took a while to get over to them because I carried out censuses of the other families on the way. When we arrived at 7:10, we saw that they were near the EAs. Enid was separated from the rest of the EBs, looking somewhat agitated, and after a few moments I realised why. Evangeline of the EAs was in oestrus, probably the early stages, since she was oestrous-walking away from several young males who were interested in her. At nine years old, Enid was young to start sexual cycling but could come into oestrus. In any event, she was following Evangeline around, fascinated by the activity.

A bull in musth was close to, but not guarding, Evangeline. This bull, estimated to be 40 years old, was named Beach Ball because he was particularly round in appearance. We had been with the family for less than five minutes when a second male in musth arrived. This was Lexi, the one-tusked bull who had so ignominiously retreated from Patrick. Lexi was about two years younger than Beach Ball but was similar to him in size. This time Lexi did not seem to be intimidated. At 7:15 I was writing some notes when Enid suddenly started screaming. I looked up and saw that she was in between Lexi and Beach Ball who were both standing tall with their ears spread and folded, threatening each other. Lexi

lunged towards Beach Ball and Enid screamed again. Other animals arrived as a result of the first scream, including Emo and Eric who stood submissively with their heads very low, watching the two musth bulls. Enid managed to extricate herself and moved off to a safe distance.

It is not unusual to see males of all ages sparring. They usually reach trunks towards each other, place them in each other's mouths, feel around each other's heads and tusks, and then gently start to push on one another. The movements in sparring are generally slow and languid, although they can escalate into more aggressive twisting and shoving. A true fight between bulls is a much rarer and very different affair involving far less physical contact and much more manoeuvring.

Beach Ball and Lexi were obviously having a serious fight despite the fact that they were not yet touching. Instead, they were manoeuvring continuously to keep facing each other at all times. If one bull turned sideways, the other could tusk him in a vulnerable area or knock him down and possibly kill him. Therefore they kept 15–20 metres (50–65 feet) apart, constantly turning and adjusting their positions with their hind legs. When they moved farther apart one or both would bash a bush or lift a large log and toss it around. Sometimes one would kneel and dig his tusks into the ground in a display that seemed to demonstrate what he would like to do to his opponent.

It was not until nearly an hour after Enid's scream that the bulls had their first clash. They came together with a tremendous thud and clank of ivory, and great clouds of dust rose from the impact. Each attempted to twist the other off his feet, but they were evenly matched and quickly backed off, resuming their lethal dance. At 8:40 they clashed again

---

When two musth males of similar age and size meet they may have a serious fight during which one could be badly injured or even killed. These fights are frightening to behold and much different in character from the almost languid sparring matches.

with the same outcome. After this Lexi found a log and stood with his front feet on it, making himself look much taller than he was. At 9:30 there was a third clash, at the end of which Beach Ball turned and started running, but then stopped and came back. Lexi went over to a large dead tree and pushed and rocked it until it fell down with a loud crash. It was a spectacular display and I thought Lexi was winning.

At 10:20 another bull, M129, arrived. He showed some signs of musth, but was only about 33 years old and therefore would not challenge the two older bulls. However, it was his lucky day. After three hours of waiting for her two suitors to finish their fight, Evangeline went off to Ol Tukai Orok with M129. At this point it was probably more important for Beach Ball and Lexi to continue their fight than to mate with one female. If the fight had a decisive ending, they would have settled their respective dominance positions and could get on with pursuing females without having to confront each other again during this musth period at least.

Beach Ball and Lexi must have been very closely matched, because the fight lasted for 10 hours and 20 minutes. During that whole time, the two bulls never fed, never drank, never relaxed. They moved farther apart or closer together but always kept facing each other. They constantly demonstrated at one another, using ear waves, emitting deep musth rumbles which we could see reverberating in their foreheads, and attacking trees, bushes and stumps. They were also dribbling urine continuously. Joyce has estimated that on a normal day a musth bull can lose as much as 400 litres (nearly 90 gallons) of water in 24 hours. This day was far from normal and by late afternoon, the two bulls must have been exhausted and dehydrated – I certainly was!

Finally at 17:35, while Beach Ball was busy beating up a dead tree, Lexi turned away. Beach Ball went after him quickly and he had to turn back. Once more Beach Ball returned to his tree, and this time Lexi turned and ran faster than any elephant I have ever seen. He went south towards the mountain with Beach Ball in hot pursuit. Just before they disappeared into the trees, we could see that Lexi was outdistancing Beach Ball and would get away. Until the very end, the fight had appeared to be a very even one but Beach Ball must have just had the edge on Lexi. Stiff and weary, Martyn and I drove back to camp for a welcome drink.

The next day was 7 June, our last day of filming in Amboseli. Although we were pleased at what we had accomplished, Martyn and I both felt very sad. Following the lives of the EBs was addictive and it would be a wrench to give it up. I, of course, would be able to see them whenever I wanted to. However, with 49 other families in Amboseli claiming my attention, I was unlikely to be able to observe the EBs in such an intimate and intensive way again. For Martyn, who was returning to the UK, the break would be much harsher. In the 17 months since he had first met the EBs he had come to know them as well as I did and care about them as much. He had a soft spot for Ella, whom he found delicate and pretty, but it was Echo's gentleness and dignity that he would never forget. Like the rest of her family we had become oriented to her, responding to her postures, gestures, moods and rhythms. In those months with her I had learned more about elephant matriarchy than I could ever have done by more traditional methods of research. In the future, those insights could be tested through scientific data collection.

It was a perfect Amboseli day with deep blue skies and Kilimanjaro standing clear and bright, completely free of clouds. The mountain dominates the landscape so much that its state seems to influence one's moods and, on this day, it quickly dispelled our sadness. We found the EBs just about to cross the road to the camp coming from the north. Echo was in the lead being the quintessential matriarch, her beautiful tusks glowing in the low morning sunlight. Everyone was there except for Emo, and, having seen him the day before, we knew he was doing fine. Disappointingly, the family moved into a large swamp just inside the palms where we could not follow them. We decided to have one last look around the park and then come back to them.

Later in the morning we returned to camp planning to approach the EBs from the other side of the swamp, but we had no need to. On our last day, the EBs had come to us. Echo and part of the family were resting under the camp tree. I took my notebooks and sat in front of my tent, relieved to be out of the vehicle after the 12-hour stint with

Above and right:

Over the 18 months the rhythm of our days was determined by the EBs as we followed them from sunrise to sunset. We had become a part of Echo's world and sometimes were privileged to feel that she and her family accepted and even welcomed our company; she taught us much about elephants, about leadship, about maternal care, survival and about some of the concepts that are not supposed to be applied to animals: patience, loyalty, love and joy.

the fighting bulls the day before. I was doing a census of the EBs when the EA family passed close by. Emerald's '89 female calf broke off from the group to join the EB calves and Ely went enthusiastically out of the family circle to meet her. After a brief exchange of trunks to each other's mouths, he started butting her with his head, and she turned and moved off. Ely put his head on her back and tried to mount, but Emerald's calf was a year older than Ely and just too tall for him. Undeterred, he reared up on his hind legs and had nearly got his feet on her back when she moved, leaving him suspended in mid-air. He took several steps forward on his back legs, looking totally ridiculous.

It was particularly interesting to watch Emerald's calf and Ely after all the adult interactions we had seen over the last two weeks. In his play, Ely had acted like a typical male calf. From very early on, male calves are more likely to leave their mothers to play and their behaviour during play is noticeably different from that of the female calves. They do more head-to-head sparring and engage in more rough and tumble play. If one calf mounts another, it will almost invariably be a male calf who does the mounting. Females tend to play running and chasing games, and those involving attacks on imaginary enemies. Both are practising skills they will need as adults: for the males, fighting and mating techniques; and for the females, strategies for protecting their calves and their families.

Ely went chasing after Emerald's calf and, even though he was now 15 months old, Enid went after him. She literally herded him back to Echo, pushing him with her trunk and tusks. He was soon off again, this time to join Ella's calf, Esau, and once again Enid followed him. She was a tireless allomother, and I felt sure she would be a good mother when she had her first calf, which could be in two or three years' time.

The elephants were soon all around my tent, ignoring me as I sat in my chair under the thatched roof. On one side, Echo, Eliot, Erin, Edgar and Eudora continued to rest under the tree. Erin was due to have a calf in a few weeks' time, and was slow and heavy. She had nearly weaned Edgar who was not at all pleased. He was only two years and eight months old, which was exceptionally young to have to go without milk. He stuck close to his mother, trying to suckle as soon as she went to sleep or got distracted, but she was on the alert and quickly stopped him. Eudora stood right next to Echo, completely integrated in the family despite her mother Emily's death. Far from becoming peripheral as I had feared, she seemed to have developed very strong bonds with Echo. I suspected that she would come into oestrous soon since she had shown some early signs of it in late May. If she did conceive in the next couple of months, she would give birth to a new calf when Elspeth was four and a half years old – much better family planning than Erin.

On the other side of my tent, Ella was feeding while six-month-old Esau played with Ely and Elspeth under a palm. Elspeth was lying down, and Ely and Esau were climbing on her and falling off. The other 'girls', Edwina, Eleanor, Emma and Enid, were standing nearby, keeping an eye on the younger calves. Eric and Ewan had joined Ebenezer and Ethan of the EAs, and they were all chasing each other through the palms.

Soon, however, most activity stopped and the members of the EBs slowly gravitated to Echo. They moved to the shade of the tree and gathered around her. The bigger animals lowered their heads, draped their trunks over their tusks, and slowly flapped their ears. The little calves flopped down and were quickly sound asleep. Even a few of the bigger calves lay down, turning into great grey boulders in the grass. Echo stood in the middle surrounded by her close relatives, each bonded to her in a different way, all dependent on her knowledge and wisdom, which had brought them through the good times and the bad.

There would be more tragedies and joys for the EBs, but for today all was peaceful, all was well.

INDEX

Page references in italics refer to illustrations